How You Can Talk to Anyone in Every Situation

Prentice Hall LIFE

If life is what you make it, then making it better starts here.

What we learn today can change our lives tomorrow. It can change our goals or change our minds; open up new opportunities or simply inspire us to make a difference. That's why we have created a new breed of books that do more to help you make more of *your* life.

Whether you want more confidence or less stress, a new skill or a different perspective, we've designed *Prentice Hall Life* books to help you to make a change for the better. Together with our authors we share a commitment to bring you the brightest ideas and best ways to manage your life, work and wealth.

In these pages we hope you'll find the ideas you need for the life *you* want. Go on, help yourself.

It's what you make it

* * *

How You Can Talk to Anyone in Every Situation

EMMA SARGENT AND TIM FEARON

Prentice Hall Life
is an imprint of

Harlow, England • London • New York • Boston • San Francisco • Toronto • Sydney • Singapore • Hong Kong
Tokyo • Seoul • Taipei • New Delhi • Cape Town • Madrid • Mexico City • Amsterdam • Munich • Paris • Milan

PEARSON EDUCATION LIMITED

Edinburgh Gate
Harlow CM20 2JE
Tel: +44 (0)1279 623623
Fax: +44 (0)1279 431059
Website: www.pearsoned.co.uk

First published in Great Britain in 2011

© Pearson Education 2011

The rights of Emma Sargent and Tim Fearon to be identified as authors of this work have been asserted by them in accordance with the Copyright, Designs and Patents Act 1988.

Pearson Education is not responsible for the content of third party internet sites.

ISBN: 978-0-273-73571-7

British Library Cataloguing-in-Publication Data
A catalogue record for this book is available from the British Library

Library of Congress Cataloging-in-Publication Data
Sargent, Emma.
  How you can talk to anyone in every situation / Emma Sargent and Tim Fearon.
    p. cm.
  ISBN 978-0-273-73571-7 (pbk.)
  1. Interpersonal communication. 2. Conversation. I. Fearon, Tim. II. Title.
  BF637.C45S265 2011
  153.6--dc22
                        2010037867

10 9 8 7 6 5 4 3 2 1
14 13 12 11 10

Typeset in 9.5/13pt Iowan Old StyleBT by 30
Printed in Great Britain by Henry Ling Ltd, at the Dorset Press, Dorchester, Dorset

Contents

About the authors

Tim Fearon

Tim's career has encompassed acting – he trained at RADA – coaching, training, conference presenting and writing.

He has formed two companies, worked with young people with significant learning difficulties, served on the board of a PLC and worked across the world with companies both large and small. And, boy, has he met a few people! Most of them absolutely brilliant – he can only think of one that he never wants to work with again.

He is a master practitioner and certified trainer of NLP as well as being a qualified hypnotherapist.

Emma Sargent

Emma balances being a parent of two with running a 'business-building for entrepreneurs' business. She has a reputation as an extremely knowledgeable, effective and inspirational speaker and works all over the world. People particularly enjoy her no-nonsense, yet warm, approach to personal and business development; she cuts through the fluff to give practical 'how to' solutions. She is less concerned with theory and more with what works.

Emma is also the author of *Brilliant Parent*. She has a psychology degree and is a certified trainer of NLP.

For the last eight years Tim and Emma have been running The Extraordinary Coaching Company. They live in the New Forest with their children, Thomas and Hannah.

You can find out about The Extraordinary Coaching Company at www.FindingTheHiddenMoney.com

Introduction

Almost all of us will experience times and situations where our confidence escapes us and we feel anxious about what to do or say.

Some of us are a bit nervous in all situations that involve people we don't know very well, others feel confident talking to one or two new faces say, but inwardly fall to pieces when faced with a large room full of strangers.

Whatever your current feelings, if you would like to feel comfortable and confident with people in any situation, you're in the right place.

This book is here to help you to become more socially confident, to enable you to engage in conversation with anyone you choose, to overcome some of the barriers that may be in the way of you being the best you can be when you are around other people and to equip you with strategies, skills and techniques to handle most social situations.

We have filled this book with practical ideas and exercises. The first two chapters give you the foundations for becoming socially confident. Chapters 3 and 4 will ensure that you are physically set up to create a really good first impression and equip you with the strategies and techniques that will allow you to enter any conversation and build fast and effective rapport with the people you meet.

In Chapters 5 and 6 we give you a whole heap of great ideas for handling issues at work and for tackling the 'difficult situations' that we all find ourselves in at one time or another. In Chapter 7, we give you all you need to know when NOT talking is the order of the day and in Chapter 8 you'll find all you need to do and say when you really want to shine!

As you read this book, we would like you to bear one thing in mind. The strategies and techniques we offer you can be used across many contexts, so think of them as being incredibly useful tools for you to take out and use whenever the need arises.

Some of the things we suggest may at first seem strange and even uncomfortable and that's only to be expected. Anything new that requires you to make a change in thinking and behaviour is pretty well bound to feel odd to start with.

If you want instant proof, try this. Cross your arms. Now uncross them and cross them the other way, so if you had your left arm on top initially, now put your right arm on top and vice versa. How does it feel? Unless you do this regularly, it'll feel a little bit strange, maybe even uncomfortable. Do it a few times more and the strangeness will go. And so it is with the 'stuff' in this book. Our only hope is that you will try things out and keep at it.

We know these techniques work. We use them ourselves and we have introduced hundreds of people to them over many years with great success.

As with any new learning, there will be those who read this book, put it aside, do little or nothing and then wonder why the techniques didn't work and nothing changed. There will be others, and our sincere hope is that you are one of them, who trust our word, take up the challenge, put them into practice and keep using them.

For you the world may become a very different one, a world filled with opportunity, enhanced relationships and the greatest gift of all; choice. The ability to choose who you talk to, when you want to and to regard every conversation as an opportunity to learn even more about this wonderful collection of beings we call the human race.

Chapter

1

The secrets of talking to anyone with confidence

We're all unique, thank heavens. How dull if we were all the same. But we do have one thing in common. We're all communicating, all the time. We're built to communicate and connect. But some of us really don't enjoy it and think we're not very good at it. And sometimes, because we don't enjoy it and think we're not very good at it, we go out of our way to avoid it.

What stops people talking to anyone in every situation with confidence?

When we've asked this question of the people we work with we've had a whole range of responses:

'I don't have anything to say.'

'I can't do small talk.'

'I stumble over my words.'

'I don't think people like me.'

'I'll say something stupid.'

'Standing up in public just scares the wits out of me.'

'No one would be interested in what I have to say.'

'I'm just not a very interesting person.'

'I dry up when people ask me questions.'

'I hate it when people look at me.'

'I don't like being around people.'

'I can't speak up with lots of people about.' ('Lots' is different for different people – pick any number you care to think of.)

When we've asked what particular situations these people find most difficult, the most common seem to be:

- meeting strangers
- dealing with people in authority – doctors, teachers, lawyers, the boss
- parties
- networking events
- social 'dos'
- making a complaint
- meetings at work
- presentations
- dealing with a difficult person/situation
- any situation when there is more than one other person present.

For some people it's a minor inconvenience, for some it's a debilitating limitation on their ability to enjoy life and for others it restricts significantly their ability to gain promotion and advance their careers. Social situations – and by social situations we mean ANYWHERE that people gather – become the bane of their lives.

So what are some of the reasons for steering clear of these situations? Well, it can be a variety of things:

- thinking that you're not interesting enough and that everyone else is better at it than you
- lack of confidence/self-esteem; sometimes triggered by a negative experience in the past
- not knowing what to do or how to do it; engage in conversation, build rapport, speak with confidence, ask questions, etc.
- anxiety/fear – worrying about what you THINK might happen.

Whichever of these most accurately reflects your own experience, this book is packed with things to help you, so let's start the ball rolling by giving you some things to think about in relation to the issues we've outlined and a couple of really powerful strategies that you can start to implement right away. We'll go into all of these in more detail later on, but we want to get you started quickly, on the basis that you probably want to do that too.

Thinking makes it happen

There's overwhelming evidence available to indicate that we get what we focus on. So, for example, if you focus on how anxious or worried you are about a situation, you tend to find that when it occurs – guess what? – you are anxious and worried!

One of the first things to do is to recognise yourself what it is that stops you speaking to anyone in any situation with confidence. If it's a matter of not knowing what to do or how to do it, the solution lies in all the strategies, tools and techniques contained in this book. Get hold of them, commit yourself to them, practise them and you will quickly find how effectively they work. You will also find that they are not 'rocket science' and do not require a degree in psychology (phew!) to implement them. They simply require application.

If it's a matter of thinking you're not good enough or a lack of confidence, then the techniques will work just as well for you, coupled with some different ways of thinking about things.

The same is true of anxiety/fear.

Catherine's story

Catherine hated it when all eyes turned on her in meetings because that made her tongue-tied and so she used never to say anything. She would get anxious before meetings, just in case anyone asked her a question and she had to respond. So we asked her, 'How do you know when to decide to become nervous?'

The question really threw her, because up to that moment she had not realised that she had any choice in the matter. She had thought that 'the nerves just take over'. But as she considered the question – we just kept asking it until she came up with an

▶

answer! – she realised that there was a moment when, as she looked at her diary for the day and saw the word 'meeting' she started to feel nervous.

And we have found this time and time again; that for anyone who suffers from a nervous or anxious reaction to a particular situation, there will be some kind of 'trigger' that starts the process. And it will always be something they see or hear. For Catherine it was seeing the word 'meeting' in her diary. And once she realised this, she also realised that she had a choice as to what she felt in that moment and decided to feel something different. How did she do that? She did the things we are going to share with you in the next chapters of this book.

And she started by doing the exercise below which you can do just before you go to any event about which you feel less than confident.

Exercise

What do you think? – Reality checker

Just before you go out, get hold of a piece of paper and a pen and divide the paper into four columns like this:

What I am thinking right now	Is it true?	Is it false?	Don't know

In the first column write down all the things you are thinking about the situation you are going into. For example, if you are going to a party where there will be some people you have never met:

'No one will want to talk to me.'

'I'm going to have an awful time.'

'They didn't really want to invite me.'

'They'll all get into groups and I won't have anyone to talk to.'

These are **only examples** – pick your own!

Then, using the next three columns, put a tick in the column that best describes your statement.

True: You have absolutely rock-solid proof for this thought or way of thinking.

False: You have incontrovertible proof that this statement is untrue.

Don't know: You don't know! You have no certain proof that it is either true or false.

You may well discover that you have less to be worried about than you thought!

We do realise that these feelings of fear and anxiety are real. We are not pretending that they just vanish overnight. What we are saying is that there is always another, and more positive, way of looking at things. There are ways of thinking that can transform our experience and there are strategies and techniques that, when applied, can make a huge difference to our ability to connect with people.

The path to social confidence

You may look at superconfident people and wonder how on earth they could be like that – and wonder what you would have to change about yourself to be that way. Would there be a danger you might start to come across as arrogant? Would you still be yourself? Would it be possible for you anyway?

The difference between someone who is socially confident and someone who is not can be distilled down into four key areas:

- know how to think
- know what you want
- know how to be confident
- know what to do.

We're going to give you an overview of these in the rest of this chapter, followed by a whole set of really powerful ways of tackling the first two – know how to think and know what you want – in Chapter 2. The rest of the book is packed with all that you need to help you to know how to be confident and know what to do.

It's going to be a great journey! We hope you enjoy it.

Know how to think – the power of beliefs

We all have a set of beliefs that act as filters to our experiences and influence our thoughts and behaviours. Socially confident people will have a different set of beliefs about meeting new people than less confident people.

The good news is that we have much more control over our beliefs and how they affect how we think and what we do than we realise. At its simplest, if we change our beliefs, we will change our behaviour.

So, what are beliefs? They are thoughts which we consider to be true and form our reality. Every experience we have is filtered through our beliefs; we pay attention to information that supports our beliefs and disregard information that does not support our beliefs. As our beliefs act as filters, our thoughts are affected by them, and so they influence our physiology, our state and our behaviour. Our beliefs have a major impact on our life. Change the unhelpful ones and you will be able to totally change how you approach and feel about social situations.

However, our beliefs are firmly rooted and remain remarkably consistent over time. This is because we are constantly, but unconsciously, looking for evidence that they are true for us. The **Belief Cycle** (Figure 1.1) demonstrates the impact that our beliefs have on our behaviour.

For example, we have worked with a lot of adults who believe that they are no good at standing up in front of a group of people to present something. Here's what is likely to happen when they are asked to make a presentation:

- **Belief**: 'I am no good at presenting.'
- **Thoughts**: 'Oh no. I wish someone else could do this for me. I hate it. It's going to be awful.'
- **State**: Nervous, anxious and butterflies in stomach.
- **Behaviour**: If you are nervous while presenting, you are likely to avoid eye contact, speak quickly and haltingly, breathe rapidly, and display a lack of engagement with your audience and lack of confidence in your message.
- **Consequences**: The audience will be disengaged and there will be a perception of you as lacking confidence and lacking conviction in your message.

As a result, your belief that you are no good at presenting will be reinforced.

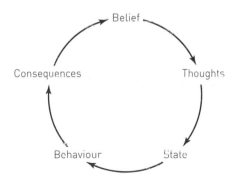

Figure 1.1 The Belief Cycle

The consequences of our behaviour therefore reinforce our beliefs, proving to us that we were right to have that belief in the first place. Here is a further example:

Richard's story

Richard believes that anyone in the service industry is out to rip him off. At some point of course that must have happened for him to form that belief in the first place, or he may have learned it from a parent or adult who was influential to him.

However, continuing to have those thoughts about everybody he meets in the service industry causes him lots of problems. Whenever he has an interaction with someone in a shop, restaurant, garage or anywhere else, he is already thinking badly of the person in front of him. His whole mind and body are set up to protect him from being ripped off. So guess what happens? He gives out lots of unconscious signals about not trusting them and they respond by doing the absolute minimum for him in terms of service. At worst, they find themselves in a position where they *feel like ripping him off.*

If you believe you are bad at something you will pay attention to examples that prove that you are right, and dismiss examples that show you are good at it. We all know someone who is determined that they are not good at something in spite of overwhelming evidence that they are. 'You don't have to be very good to get to Grade 8 on the flute', a friend said recently, having got to Grade 8. Oh really?

Some people's beliefs are so strongly entrenched, that other people get sucked into them. We know someone who absolutely believes that other people will not do what she wants them to do for her. All her attention goes into thinking that they won't deliver their promises. Because of her behaviour, we found ourselves in a position recently with her where we felt like not doing what we had agreed to do for her!

Whatever you believe, either positively or negatively, you will be proved right.

What then are the beliefs that we have discovered to be held by socially confident people? Here's a list of some of them:

- meeting people is fun
- meeting people means that I will learn new things
- all people are different and that means it's going to be interesting
- everyone has something unique to offer
- people like to be listened to
- it's always possible to find something we have in common
- everyone has a story worth telling
- whilst some people may appear 'difficult', there's always a positive intention (positive for them) behind their behaviour
- I have something to contribute to every conversation.

Know what you want – four secrets for success

Ask any person who demonstrates success in any area of human endeavour and they will tell you that they have, and always have had, a very clear idea of what they wanted.

Having worked over the years with many successful people, including some highly effective and confident communicators, we have discovered that they all operate in a similar way. They follow the four success guidelines outlined below:

Firstly, they think about what they **do** want, **not** what they **don't** want.

Secondly, they mentally rehearse having it already.

Thirdly, they think about the consequences of getting it, positive and negative, to themselves and those around them.

Fourthly, they make sure that they can take action themselves, and that someone else is not responsible for the action.

Let's consider them in turn.

Successful people think about what they do want, not what they don't want

Have you ever told yourself not to do something? Try it now. Tell yourself not to think of a pink elephant. What happens? You'll probably notice that you had to think of the elephant before not thinking about it!

Why is this so important? It's important because 'not' occurs in language but not in our thoughts. So if we tell ourselves not to do something, we have to think of that something first. And when we do that, we are instructing our mind to think of the very thing that we don't want.

Think for a minute about the following statements:

'I mustn't eat cake today.'

'I don't want to lose my temper with my boss.'

'I must be careful not to slip.'

'I don't want to run out of things to say.'

As you read these statements, what images come to mind? Eating cake, having an argument, slipping over and running out of things to say, probably! Whatever you imagine happening acts as an instruction to your unconscious mind to do it.

"We can't not think about what we don't want to think about until we have thought about it first!"

It is much more effective to give yourself the following instructions as alternatives to the above statements:

'I will eat healthy food today.'

'I will be calm and positive with my boss today.'

'I will walk carefully.'

'I will always have something to add to the conversation.'

With these statements, you will imagine what you **do** want, rather than what you don't.

Take a moment to think about whether generally you think about what you **do** want to happen or what you **don't** want to happen. It makes a big difference.

Tip: Start thinking about what you DO want. Write it down; it can have a major impact on your thinking and on your life.

Successful people mentally rehearse having it already

The great boxer Mohammad Ali is a wonderful example in this respect. He created something he called 'Future History'.

As soon as he knew who his next opponent was to be, let's say Sonny Liston at Madison Square Gardens on 4 November, he would lock himself away and start to prepare.

He would rehearse the whole fight in his mind from the moment he arrived at the Gardens on the night of the fight right the way through his dressing room preparation, the walk into the ring, the fight and his eventual victory.

In order to build it 'into the muscle' he would also rehearse it physically, practising the punches he would throw, the moves he would make.

Once he had it rehearsed, he would then run it repeatedly until he could run the whole thing in his mind in seconds. He would then appear before the assembled press and say, 'He falls in four'. His predictions had a spooky way of coming true.

Of course, at some point he lost and when questioned by a reporter who challenged the power of his 'future history' he simply replied, 'The other guy's future history was stronger than mine!' A great example of a champion who believed that victory is mostly in the mind.

Successful people think about the consequences of getting it, both positive and negative, to themselves and those around them

In other words, does what they want fit with who they are and what's important to them? They put themselves even further into the future and ask themselves, 'What will happen when I get what I want? Will I lose anything that I have now? How will it impact on those around me and is it worth it?'

These consequences play a huge role in our motivation to reach our goal. If the consequences are not compelling for us, we don't feel motivated to take action. If we actively think through all the consequences, in this case of becoming socially confident, we will be highly motivated to take action and make the changes we need to.

How would it feel to be able to walk into any room and be completely at ease, whoever was there? What would the consequences be for your life?

Successful people make sure that they can take action themselves, and that someone else is not responsible for the action

We are only responsible for our own behaviour. We can't set an outcome for someone else to behave in a certain way and expect it to happen.

We have to look to ourselves first. What can **we** do differently that will make it more likely that the other person will behave differently towards us?

Know how to be confident

We have already said that thinking a certain way leads to certain behaviours. You saw in the Belief Cycle in Figure 1.1 that our thoughts have an impact on how we feel first, and it is how we feel that leads to the way we behave.

Socially confident people are able to manage their emotional state so that even if they feel nervous they don't look it.

In fact it would be more accurate to say that our behaviour is entirely dependent on, and the result of, our emotional state. We will show you in the next chapter how you can change your emotional state by thinking differently.

Confident people always appear confident. You will probably know, or at least have seen, people who exude confidence in a social setting. So, here's a question for you to consider: How do you know they're confident?

We're going to be 'unpacking' confidence a little later in the book and in the meantime, try this exercise.

Exercise

What is confidence?

Write down your answers to the question, 'How do you know that someone is confident?'

What are their characteristics? What have you noticed them say or do that makes you believe they are confident?

Keep your list somewhere handy; you'll need it later.

Know what to do – the rules of engagement

Lastly, there is the actual knowledge of what to do and how to be an effective communicator in a whole variety of situations, including the following:

- how to engage in conversation
- how to get your point across
- how to stand up for yourself
- how to come across in the way you want to
- how to listen
- how to express interest in others

- how to make people feel good
- how to deal with 'difficult' situations and people
- how to get the most out of the events you attend
- how to build rapport quickly and effectively
- how to connect with people on a deeper level.

Having identified what confident conversationalists do, now's the time to apply their strategies for success to ourselves.

Chapter

2

It's all about you

By the end of this chapter you will have a very good understanding of how to create a powerfully confident state before entering any room or meeting any person.

You might be thinking, 'This is a strange place to start helping me to talk to anyone in every situation. Can't we just get on with the things I need to do?' Well, we could have done that but here's the thing. Your ability to implement the strategies and techniques that we are going to give you will be hugely enhanced when you are able to do that in a state of confidence. Doing anything confidently is likely to significantly increase your chances of success.

But where does confidence come from; what helps us to be confident and what gets in the way?

Given the extraordinarily powerful influence of our beliefs on our thinking, our state and our behaviour, it makes sense to start our journey of exploration here.

Know how you think – harness the power of beliefs

If you want to become a really confident communicator you need to have an understanding of what goes on in your head – and what goes on in other people's heads: how you and other people process information and organise their thoughts to create their unique internal world, and hence their unique view of the external world.

Why is it important to understand it? Because once you understand how you create your own thoughts and internal experiences, it means that you have the choice to change them if you want to.

So many people we work with believe they have no choice. Similarly to Catherine in Chapter 1, they tell us that, 'It's just the way I am. I've never been any good at socialising/talking to people in senior positions/getting my point across/being assertive/enjoying parties/talking in a group.' And they believe that that's the way it's always going to be.

Well, if that strikes a chord with you, we have great news for you. You can change and you can change easily, if you want to. But in order to change, you first need to understand how you are creating the thoughts and feelings that you have at the moment. And that's the purpose of this part of the book. When you understand this process you will know:

- how you make sense of all the information around you
- how you filter the information around you
- how you create your thoughts
- how your thoughts interact with your physiology to create emotions
- how your emotions affect your behaviour
- how most of this process happens unconsciously.

Our senses are bombarded with information. In every moment, millions upon millions of pieces in the form of sights, sounds, touch, taste and smell surround us. However, we can only pay attention, consciously, to approximately seven pieces of information at once, give or take two. That is, we can pay attention to five pieces on a bad day and nine on a good day. Do you remember playing the memory game as a child? Up to twenty random items were put on a tray and you had a few minutes to memorise them. It was rare that anyone remembered more than eight or nine items.

Try it for yourself. How about attempting to name all the alcoholic drinks you can think of. Just think about that yourself for a few moments.

What happened? If your experience is anything like ours you probably found that you thought of a few very quickly – between five and nine – and then had to think before the next group came to mind. You may also have found that the drinks came to you in clusters, e.g. spirits, wines, beers, etc.

So, we are bombarded with millions of pieces of information in every moment, and yet we can only consciously pay attention to a very small number. What happens to all the rest? We simply **delete** it. In fact we have to delete it or our internal computer would overload and crash.

We also **distort** the information in order for it to make sense to us. Have you ever been somewhere with a friend and realised afterwards that you had very different experiences? You have both been in the same place at the same time, and when you talk about it afterwards, you can't quite believe that you were!

Thirdly, we **generalise** the experience. Generalisation is the process by which we learn. Once, as a child, we have learned how to open a door, we generalise our experience of opening a few doors and apply it to all doors. Just imagine what would happen if we had to learn how to open the door every time we came across one!

So, all our experiences are subject to three internal processes: deletion, distortion and generalisation.

And as we do all these things, the really important question is, what exactly DO we pay attention to? It depends on the filters through which we view the experience. And what are filters? Our filters include our beliefs and values, memories, our preferences and interests; in short, all the coding of our past and present experience.

All this filtering happens outside of our conscious awareness.

To recap: we have an experience and we sift all the information through our filters which have been formed throughout our lives from our life experiences. These filters inform what we pay attention to in order to turn millions of pieces of information into a few. As a result of the filtering, we form our internal representation (thoughts) of the experience in our minds.

This **internal representation** is made up of images (Visual), sounds (Auditory), feelings (Kinaesthetic), tastes and smells. We have internal representations which are memories and we also create new ones for events that haven't happened yet, known as our imagination.

And it is a person's internal representations that will determine how they experience every event in their lives. Sometimes this will allow them to achieve success; sometimes it will limit them.

Here's an **example** of how this works: Let's create an internal representation right now to demonstrate. Imagine you are going to an event where you are unlikely to know many people and you will be expected to mix and mingle. What is the image that comes to mind? What thoughts go along with it? What sounds are associated with the image?

Firstly, your internal representation of this event will be informed by any similar previous experiences you have had. It will also be filtered through your beliefs about such events – do you think they are fun, or are they to be avoided at all costs? And it will also be filtered through your beliefs about yourself in relation to the people who may be there; do you think they will be welcoming or do you think they may huddle in groups of people that already know each other?

So, your internal representation is made up of images, sounds, feelings and perhaps tastes and smells.

These thoughts affect our demeanour, our **physiology**. If you are dreading the event you will look different and hold yourself differently from someone who is excited about it.

Conversely, our physiology affects our thoughts too. If you stand tall and breathe deeply you are more likely to have positive thoughts about standing up in front of a group of people than if you hunch your shoulders and look at the floor.

> **Internal representation + physiology = state**

Your internal representation combined with your physiology is called your **state** or emotion. Here are two examples:

Example 1

I am going to a networking event where there are going to be a lot of people I have never met before. My internal representation is this: I am imagining a group of people smiling, enjoying themselves, being very open and welcoming. I can hear them talking animatedly. I am imagining myself making new connections easily. I see myself with a small group of them, discussing future possibilities of co-operation and doing business together.

As I am having these thoughts, I start to smile and I get a warm feeling in my chest. I begin to feel excited.

Example 2

I am going to a networking event. I am thinking about a group of business people (very senior) who all appear to know each other. They are talking loudly together in groups and I am not sure how to make contact as the groups are closed off. I am the only person standing on my own. I am not sure that they will pay attention to me if I try to introduce myself into a group.

As I am having these thoughts, my head drops, my shoulders droop and my breathing becomes shallow. I begin to feel worried.

Your internal representation has an incredibly strong influence. If you have a 'glass half empty' filter, you may be paying attention to what is not right in your life. Your internal representations may be of things going wrong. If you think about things constantly going wrong in your life, your physiology is likely to be downcast and you are likely to feel anxious, worried or even depressed for some of the time. If you spend time in that state, how likely is it that things will go right for you?

If you have a 'glass half full' filter, you are more likely to pay attention to what is going right in your life. Your internal representations will be of things working out for you which will result in a positive demeanour and a positive feeling. If you feel and act positively, it is more likely that things will go right in your life.

If you want to give yourself the best chance of achieving something, however small, it is really useful to imagine a picture of your achieving it. For example:

- if you have just moved into a new home and have been invited to a neighbour's house to meet a group of local people, imagine them welcoming you and making you feel at home
- if you have a meeting with your boss to go to, imagine it going well
- if you are going to meet a group of strangers at a networking event, imagine them smiling at you and having a good time
- if you want to make a really good presentation to a group of colleagues or a client imagine them paying attention to you and being really engaged.

If you do this, you are more likely to get what you imagine as you are setting up your whole system to get it: you have the internal representation of getting it, your physiology will be positive and that will mean that you feel positive and motivated too. If you feel positive and motivated, you give yourself the best chance of behaving in a way that means you will achieve your outcome.

State and behaviour

The state that you experience as a result of your thoughts will affect your behaviour. Your state always affects your behaviour.

Back to the networking event; how are you likely to behave if you are concerned about it and worried about attending? How might you behave differently if you are excited and looking forward to it? You are more likely to notice the positive reactions of the attendees if you are being positive yourself, because it is what you are paying attention to.

Being able to manage your state is a vital skill for life. In the next section we're going to look at some really effective ways to do that.

Know what you want

Exercise

You today

Take a few moments to write down your beliefs about yourself in a social situation:

- How do you see yourself?
- How would you describe yourself?
- How do you think people would describe you?

Now get hold of the list you made in Chapter 1 of the characteristics of socially confident people you know or have observed.

Exercise

You and confidence

Take time to compare the results from the first two exercises and note your responses:

- What differences do you notice?
- What characteristics of the socially confident people are you most keen to develop?

If your list of the characteristics of those really confident people is anything like those that people we work with generate, then you will probably have on it words like:

charisma, personality, holds attention, clear, relaxed, good voice, humorous, easy to listen to, knowledgeable, calm, connects with the people they're talking to, etc.

And sometimes it can look like a pretty daunting list. But the key to discovering the secrets of these amazing communicators is not to be overawed by the apparent size of the challenge, but to go behind the labels and find out what is really going on.

"Think about what you want, not what you don't want."

Exercise

Creating the future 'you'

You are now about to decide what you want to become in the situations in which you want to become more confident. You are about to frame a compelling outcome.

Why is this so important? Because there is so much evidence to support the idea that those people who set themselves clear, compelling, rich and detailed outcomes are far more likely to achieve them than those people who don't. And any great communicator that you talk to will have ready answers to the questions below.

Find a quiet place and give yourself plenty of time to do this exercise. Ask yourself these questions:

- When you're there in the situations in which you want to become more confident, how do you want to be seen?
- What kind of impact do you want to have on people?
- How do you want the people you meet and talk with, to experience and describe you?
- How will you know that you have achieved your outcome?
- What commitment are you ready to make to achieve your outcome?

Mentally rehearse having it

As you consider these questions we want you to fully associate with the future you are creating. Sit comfortably, relax, close your eyes if it helps you. Take yourself into the future and imagine yourself in one of the situations in which you want to be able to speak to everyone with confidence, doing exactly that.

- What do you see around you?
- How are the people reacting to you?
- See the smiles on their faces, the nods of agreement, their obvious interest in you.
- Notice how easy it is for them to listen to you and how easy it is for you to keep your attention completely on them.
- What are they saying to you?
- What questions do they have that demonstrate their interest and understanding in what you have said?
- Listen to their wonderfully positive comments. How does all this make you feel?
- Notice how relaxed and confident you are in their presence.
- Be aware how much enjoyment you are able to get from the positive impact you are clearly having on them.

This is the start of your journey towards becoming a great communicator!

Using this exercise every day

We suggest that you do this last exercise every day. You need only spend 5–10 minutes going through it; it will make a positive, noticeable difference to your levels of confidence.

Use this time for you to make this experience as rich and rewarding as you can, knowing that it is all completely achievable. And when you have finished, run through it two or even three times more, each time allowing it to become easier and easier until you can re-create and run through the experience as quickly as you like whenever you want to.

And as you do this exercise, think about your purpose. Whatever situation or situations you find most challenging at the moment, this exercise will help you to set the scene for your eventual, confident success.

Now let's step further into the future:

"Think about the consequences of getting it."

> ### Exercise
>
> Consequences
> - What are the long-term consequences of your ability to talk to everyone with confidence?
> - What is going to be the positive impact of this on you and on the people who you are with?
> - Is there anything that could get in the way of you achieving this and, if there is, what do you need to do to overcome it?

"Make sure that you can take action yourself, and that someone else is not responsible for your actions."

If you are to become the confident communicator that you want to be, you have to recognise that the responsibility for achieving it rests solely with you. Whilst we can give you strategies that we know work, whilst friends and colleagues may be able to give you help and useful advice, the only person who can effect the changes is you.

All the most successful people, in any walk of life, are those who put themselves 'at cause'. In other words they take responsibility for what happens to them and for the responses and reactions they have to what happens in their lives.

They recognise that at each and every moment in their lives they have a choice. They have a choice as to how they react to events; as to how they react to people. Knowing this and acting on it are attributes of the truly confident person.

Making the changes

So how do we get from where we are now to where we want to be?

You have already made the first step by setting yourself a future 'you' to focus on. As it is now in your conscious awareness it is more likely to happen. Why? Because in your mind, you have already rehearsed being the best you can be.

Now you're going to take all the great work you've done and apply it to the various situations in which you want to be even more confident.

But just before you do that, take a few moments to consider this:

> **Conversation n.** the interchange through speech of information, ideas, etc.; spoken communication
> (*Collins English Dictionary*)
>
> **Synonyms:** chat, chinwag, debate, dialogue, discourse, discussion, gossip, powwow, talk, tête-à-tête, heart to heart, natter.

Have a look at these words and notice the response that you get. Do some of them give you different feelings from others? If we invited you to debate something with a group of people, would that make you feel different from if we'd asked you to chat about it? If you were asked to have a discussion as opposed to a heart to heart, would that be different?

Start to become aware of the feelings you get that are generated by the way something is described. We work a lot with people who want to eradicate their fear of giving business presentations.

*Tip: If you have the same problem, start thinking of them as **conversations** and see what happens. Simply asking some of our clients to do this has made the most enormous difference to their attitude and confidence.*

It's the same with all sorts of different social situations. What happens to you when you think about going to:

- a party?
- a client meeting?
- a social gathering?
- an office 'do'?
- a banquet?
- a dinner party?
- a bit of a get together?
- a charity event?
- a ball?
- a conference?
- a seminar?
- a networking event?
- an external training course?

Do you notice any differences? We're going to guess that you do, and it's in the differences that the issues of social confidence occur.

Exercise

Making the changes

So to complete the exercise, take those situations – they may be in this list and you may have others you want to add – in which you want to become more confident, and apply the principles of the 'Creating the future "you"' exercise to it.

For example, if you have a dinner party coming up that you are apprehensive about, then use this as the context and run through the exercise exactly as you have practised it already.

Top tips for getting rid of anxiety

1. **Make an image of the event going well**: We've talked about that already in some detail.

2. **Push the negative image away**: Think of the situation you are walking into, or the person you are going to be meeting that causes you anxiety. Make as clear a picture of this as you can. Then start to push the picture away from you and as it grows smaller start to notice the difference it makes to your feelings and your state.

3. **Get confident**: We're going to give you some terrific ways of generating and maintaining confidence in Chapter 3.

Chapter

3

Conversation basics

If the thought of having to start a conversation with strangers makes you feel distinctly anxious, don't worry. The chances are that you don't have any problem talking to your friends. So remember that; there was a time when you didn't know the people that you now feel most at ease with. In fact, aside from family every relationship you have started has been with a stranger. It follows then that every social event is an opportunity to meet people who may become friends.

So now the question is, what can you do to set yourself up to have a good time whatever the event and what are some of the strategies you can employ that will ensure you have the best time possible?

First things first

We already know that one thing that marks out the most successful communicators is that they always have an outcome in mind. So if we apply this to ourselves it translates into a very simple question: **What do you want?**

What do you want to get out of any event that you attend? When you leave the event, how will you know you have achieved your outcome? This can sound a bit formalised or businesslike but you really can apply it to anything. For example:

- A party – it might be just a real determination and focus on enjoying yourself.
- An office 'do' – speaking to at least three people from different parts of the business.
- A dinner party – deciding to find out at least one thing you never knew about all the other guests.

- A charity event – finding out as much as you can about the charity and the way it is organised.
- A ball – dancing with at least one person that you do not know.
- A conference – making five new connections and speaking to at least one of the speakers whose subjects most interest you.
- A networking event – deciding, once you have seen the attendance list, exactly who you want to connect with.
- An external training course – learning and being on first-name terms with three to five of the other attendees by lunchtime on the first day.

And you don't need to stretch yourself too far. Give yourself something to aim for and that in itself will allow you to focus on other people rather than on yourself and any uncertainty or nervousness that you used to feel.

The secret to being interesting

Surprisingly, the people who are regarded as the most interesting and who get invited back tend to be those who are interested in others, not those who go on and on about themselves. You'll have heard of, and probably even met, people who could 'bore for Britain'. Well, you never want to be seen as one of those, do you?

So get curious about people, about their backgrounds, about their lives, about their loves. There's nothing that makes people feel more flattered and want to spend more time with you. Have you ever had that experience, where you've been made to feel like the most fascinating person in the room? How did it make you feel?

We were talking a little while ago to a friend of ours, Julie, who, the evening before, had been to a party with her boyfriend, David.

'What was it like?' we asked.

'Oh, great for David!' was her slightly acerbic response.

'What happened?'

'Well, when we got there, we split up as we tend to do, to talk to different friends. I usually end up talking to the girls and David to the lads.

When we'd been there a while, I noticed him talking to one woman, Vanessa, that I hadn't met before who was absolutely gorgeous! I became slightly concerned! Then a little while later I saw him deep in conversation with another woman, Sue, who I had met fleetingly and who, to be frank, was a lot less glamorous. To cut a long story short, I hardly saw him all evening and when I did see him, he was with other women!

Anyway, on the way home I asked him how he had enjoyed the evening.

"Yeah, really good."

"So, what did you think of Vanessa?" I asked.

"She's OK, but Sue ... wow! What a fabulous woman!"

Well, I was surprised, to say the least.

"So what makes her so fabulous?"

"I don't know, I guess she's just so interesting."

But when I asked David what made her so interesting, I found out that he knew very little about her. But guess what? She knew everything about him! It sounded like it had been an almost entirely one way conversation. Poor, interesting, woman!'

A small story that illustrates a hugely important point:

"Being interested makes you interesting!"

And that means that if we stay focused on **being interested** and finding out about people, we run the risk of becoming very popular! And it makes it a whole lot easier than thinking we have to have 1487 interesting things to say whenever we meet other people. Phew, what a relief!

When it comes to social settings, we sometimes get too caught up in the idea that it's all about what we say; that we are judged by our output; that being interesting is inextricably linked to our ability to amuse, entertain and hold court. Believe us, there are very, very, very few people in our experience who can do those three things with anything like success.

Of course, there are people who can do it, but they are few and far between and have a set of skills and abilities that are more likely to be a result of nature rather than nurture.

For the rest of us, it's a matter of learning some really useful strategies, implementing them and practising them on a regular basis. If you think about it, it's pretty much the same with any skill. How many really good, successful, sportspeople do you think get there simply by virtue of just natural ability? And how many do you think get there by dedicated practice? How many actors do you think go on stage without rehearsal? The world doesn't work that way. And if practise and rehearsal do it for them, maybe we should take a leaf out of their book.

So let's start by looking at some of the strategies that will help us in any social situation.

Starting points

Most people we know who feel less than confident in social settings tell us that one of their biggest concerns is having something to say. And they get so concerned about this that when the time comes to speak, they simply dry up. In fact someone we were talking to recently said, 'It's just as if my head empties and I can't find any of the words I need.'

Well, if we go back to our thoughts on successful sportspeople and actors, the first lesson we learn is that the three secrets of a great performance are: 'Rehearse, Rehearse, Rehearse'. And while we're not necessarily aiming to 'perform', there's wisdom in their method. So let's start rehearsing!

Think of any situation where you are going to meet new people. (We'll look at this first as these are the situations that people usually find most difficult.) What kind of questions are you most likely to be asked? Well, probably:

- Who are you?
- What do you do?
- Where do you live?
- How do you know Paul and Molly?

Exercise

Write your autobiography

Before we start to examine these questions in more detail, here's what we want you to do:

Write your autobiography!

Just take a pen and paper, find yourself a quiet half hour or so, and write out your life story. You're not looking for *War and Peace*; you're just looking to record the main events of your life. And don't think about it too much, just let the thoughts flow.

Tim was working with someone a couple of years ago who, over a couple of drinks one evening, asked him about his life; how he came to be doing what he was doing, etc. Now, Tim's not a great one for talking about himself, so he said something along the lines of, 'How long have you got?' hoping she would drop the subject. But she persisted and so he gave her a potted version of the life of Tim. At the end she looked at him and said, 'Wow, you've had an amazing life, haven't you?'

Now Tim had never thought of his life as amazing; it's just his life. But from her perspective it was amazing. And here's something you should always remember; no one else has lived your life and even if you think you've had a relatively mundane existence, you should never assume that everyone else will see it in the same way.

So, stop reading and get on with your homework! And when you've finished, take a few moments to reflect on it and start to notice the parts of your life that you can take into any conversation. You have a story and if there's one thing that people love, it's stories.

And, of course, different parts of your story will be of interest to different people. So spend a bit more time thinking through in what environments and at what events you will be able to use the different parts of your story.

If it helps you, then write them out in a bit more detail so that when the time comes, you have plenty to tell.

Now let's turn our attention to the questions that you so often get asked.

'Who are you?'

Interesting fact: lots of people don't answer this question. They do give an answer but often it's the answer to the question, 'What do you do?' The reason? Their job becomes the way in which they identify themselves. Their sense of worth is derived from what they do rather than who they are.

This, then, is an opportunity for you to make an impression that is totally unique because there is only one of you whereas there are quite a few people who work in offices!

Do it yourself/rehearsal time

So take a few moments now to work out what you want to say about yourself.

Hint: 'I'm Jill/Jack' really isn't good enough! You want to give the other person enough information for them to be able to respond to and/or ask you more about yourself.

And think what you would like the other person to say when they are asked later, 'Who was that fascinating/intriguing/interesting/gorgeous/handsome/charismatic (choose the one you like best!) person I saw you talking to?'

What have you got? OK, name is fine and, in fact, essential as it is the first piece of information that enables you to start to build some level of rapport. Using people's names is a great way to begin the process of building a relationship with them. You know only too well the pulling power of your own name. Have you ever been talking to someone at a party when someone else in another group has used your name and it seems to cut through the air like a knife? And they may not even be talking about you; it's just the sound of your name that immediately gets your attention.

So what other information can you offer besides your name? Firstly think about the situation you're in and then consider what would be the most appropriate information to give that could spark a conversation. Here are some examples:

Party: 'I'm Tim and I've just moved in next door.'

Office 'do': 'I'm Mary and I work in the other building in Finance.'

Dinner party: 'I'm Peter, a work colleague of Martin's. First time he's ever invited me over!'

Conference: 'I'm Louise from ABC Widgets. I'm really looking forward to the next speaker.'

What you've done here is to give the other person a hook to latch on to. You can always finish off with, 'And what about you?' which neatly puts the ball back in their court and also makes sure you aren't going on about yourself too much!

'What do you do?'

Once again, rehearsal is the key and your response will depend on the situation you find yourself in.

Homework/rehearsal

How are you going to describe what you do? 'I'm in sales' isn't going to get you very far. Neither is 'I'm a brain surgeon.' Although, to be fair, it will probably get you further than 'I'm a reinsurance intermediary.'

So, spice it up a bit. Make your description more than the job title.

Let's do some examples:

'I'm a mother with 1/2/3/4 children which is a cross between running a B&B and managing a counselling service.'

'I help people with no grasp on financial reality to keep their affairs in order.' (Accountant)

'I do something that accountants find a little bit too exciting.' (Reinsurance Intermediary)

'I spend most of the day wondering why I do it.' (Dentist – but that's just our view of the job. Actually most dentists we know refuse to admit it to strangers as they tend to end up being asked for an on the spot consultation!)

'I'm a builder, and yes, I turn up on time and finish the job on time! But then I'm very unusual.'

Or just add something onto your job that gives the other person a chance to extend the conversation:

'I work in the health service and it's never been tougher to meet our budgets.'

The thing to do here is to consider, bearing in mind the situation you're in, what sort of information would be useful for your listener/s and could therefore spark their interest and a conversation. In other words, make your comments relevant to your audience.

So, if you're attending a business conference and meet a business owner:

'I work for a mortgage broker and we do a lot of work in the commercial sector.'

If you were at a party, you might change that to:

'I work for a mortgage broker. We've got a good presence in the house market although things are pretty tough at the moment.'

'Where do you live?'

Same rules apply; add something to your answer.

> 'Redditch' doesn't cut the mustard!

> 'We live in Basingstoke and, heaven help us, we've been there for twenty years.'

> 'We live in the New Forest. If you love the countryside and the sea, it's a great place to be.'

> 'We live in Birmingham. More parks than Paris; more canals than Venice.' (All true, by the way.)

'How do you know Paul and Molly?'

We hope you're getting the hang of it by now:

> 'We were at school together. I never dreamed he would join the Army.'

> 'We used to live next door to them just after they got married. We all loved the area. Do you know Leeds at all?'

We've now introduced another great strategy to move the conversation on; **the question** at the end of your answer that hands the baton back to your companion. And if you review all the example answers above, you'll see how you could use this strategy with every one of them:

> 'We live in the New Forest. If you love the countryside and the sea, it's a great place to be. Have you ever been there?'

> 'I work in the health service and it's never been tougher to meet our budgets. What are things like in your business?'

By doing this, you have made it really easy for the other person to answer and for you to pick up on another area of your answer if the conversation falters. In the New Forest example, you've given your companion the opportunity to pick up the New Forest, the countryside or the sea.

If, however, they simply answer, 'No' (see the section about types of questions – you have asked a closed question) you then have the opportunity to come back with a question about either the countryside or the sea. You could even bounce off into a question about holidays:

'Of course, a lot of people come down to the Forest for their holidays. What are you doing this year?/Where do you like to holiday?/Where did you go for your holidays last year?' You now have a lot of options and that's a great position to be in.

Keeping it going – listening

So, once you've got things going, the next challenge is **keeping it going!**

The first rule of keeping things flowing is to focus on your companion/s. Keeping things flowing is relatively easy once you stop becoming concerned about it and once you focus on what the other person is saying.

The reason so many people find this difficult is that they get too tied up in thinking what to say next. You'll get loads of clues of what to say next as long as you **listen.**

Now, it goes without saying that listening is one of the most important skills to have. The interesting thing is that, of all the language skills we need in our lives, it is the one that is never taught! How many times do you remember, as a child, being asked, 'Why on earth don't you listen?' or 'Don't you ever listen?' or sometimes not being asked at all, just told, 'Will you listen!' The fact is though that we were never taught to listen.

So what does listening – really effective listening – entail? If you want to know the answer to that, take a look at the Chinese interpretation:

Undivided
attention

Ear   Eye

King   Heart

For the Chinese, then, listening involves us paying undivided attention to the other person. It means that we listen with every part of us. It means that the other person becomes the centre of our world and that we focus entirely on them to the exclusion of everything else. And that's not easy!

- How often have you found yourself drifting off while the other person is talking?
- How often have you found yourself having to ask the other person to repeat themselves because you missed what they said?
- How many times have you been asked a question that has completely stumped you because you missed the run up to it?
- How many times have you found yourself thinking about your shopping list/next holiday/whether you switched all the lights off/what you're doing next weekend/a problem at work, while someone else is speaking?

If you have ever experienced any of these, **you have not been listening**!

So, if you really want to be able to talk to anyone with confidence, first become an expert listener. Not only will you be valued more as a friend, as a guest, as a colleague; you will also grow in confidence, knowing that since you are listening you will be able to pick up as much, and probably a lot more, than you will ever need to keep a conversation flowing.

So, how do you listen and what helps you to listen?

- Do whatever you can to 'stop the noise' – those are the other thoughts that come into your head when others are speaking.
- Concentrate totally on the speaker and what is being said.
- Avoid the temptation of starting to prepare your reply before they have finished.
- Listen with an open mind and an open heart – remember the Chinese symbol.
- Avoid assumptions and rushing to judgement.

- Give visual encouragement to the speaker – make good eye contact, smile, nod.

- Give verbal and vocal encouragement to the speaker – use phrases such as 'yes', 'I see', 'I understand' or even just sounds like 'mmm' or 'ah'.

- Don't interrupt.

- Don't rush to fill a silence.

- If you want to be sure that you've understood a particular point, reflect it back to the speaker and check that this really is what they meant.

- When you want to remember a detail, repeat it immediately.

And talking of repetition, repetition is in itself another great strategy for keeping things going. It's very simple and here's how it works.

All you need to do is to **listen carefully** to what is being said and repeat one or some of the key words that the other person uses. And as you do this, use a questioning tone in your voice. For example:

> **Them**: 'I went to an awful party last week.'
> **You**: 'Awful?'

> **Them**: 'I really don't get why people enjoy going to the gym.'
> **You**: 'You don't get it?'

> **Them**: 'I saw the new Bond film the other day. It was brilliant.'
> **You**: 'Brilliant?'

> **Them**: 'Business hasn't been great for quite a while.'
> **You**: 'Not been great?'

All of these questions are aimed at getting the other person to expand on their experience. The other effect is to demonstrate, by using their words and phrases, that you have been listening and that you are interested in what they have been saying.

Tip: You must ALWAYS use the other person's words. Don't interpret or use your own words or phrases. Using their words really adds power and is the ultimate proof of your listening.

Now, on the page, some of this can look a little odd; but it does work. Try it and see.

Keeping it going – questioning

"The information that you want is in the question you intend to ask.**"**
Jiddu Krishnamurti

So far we've talked about keeping things going through repetition and using a questioning inflection and now it's time to turn to questioning itself. There is an art to asking questions and fortunately it's an art that is easy to learn. And the more you practise it, the easier it will become.

Now you may be familiar with questioning techniques, or they may be new to you. Whichever position you are in, that's fine because if you know about them, it's always great to review and refresh things. If you're not familiar with them, then you're in for a treat!

Basically, there are two types of questions: open and closed. We're going to look at both types and identify when to use them to get the best results.

Closed questions are questions that usually generate short, influenced answers, often 'Yes' or 'No'. For example:

'Do you come here often?' (Sorry, couldn't resist it!)

'Are you friends of the family?'

'Have you known them for long?'

'Are you going anywhere for Christmas?'

'Will you be watching the match on TV tonight?'

So you'll see that typically they begin with words like: can, do, are, is, have, would, should, did, will, etc.

Now we know people who, if you ask them a closed question, are still talking three hours later, but by and large closed questions tend not to get you a lot of information.

That doesn't mean they're not good questions. It just means that if you want to keep the conversation going, they're not the best questions to use. They are best used for specific reasons, like confirming information or to bring things to a conclusion:

'Does that mean you've decided to go to Greece next summer?'

'Is it time to get ready to go?'

'Didn't you have time to get the shopping?'

'Will you be able to collect the kids from school?'

Open questions come in two forms that are well worth understanding and getting familiar with. But before we go on to look at these in more detail, let's just identify the words to use that **always** start an open question. They are: what, when, where, who, how, why, which.

"I have six serving men and true; they taught me all I know. Their names are what and where and when and how and why and who.**"**
Rudyard Kipling

Presumably Kipling didn't include 'which' because if he had, his poem wouldn't have rhymed!

The other method of getting great information is to use, 'Tell me ...'

'Tell me about your holiday.'

'Tell me how you got on.'

'Tell me more.'

The two forms of open questions are:

- **Open neutral.**
- **Open leading.**

Open neutral questions tend to generate long **uninfluenced** answers. These are questions that give the other person the most choice about what to say in response.

So, imagine someone you are talking to tells you they have just come back from a holiday in France. A great open neutral question would be: 'How was your holiday?' or 'How was it?' or, using the 'Tell me ...' approach, 'Tell me about it.'

Using this strategy gives your companion the opportunity to tell you anything they want about their holiday. You have not influenced them in any way.

If, on the other hand, you want to find out about a particular aspect of their holiday, then use an open leading question. **Open leading** questions tend to generate long, **influenced** answers. These questions lead the other person to talk about the subject area that **you want them** to talk about. If we take the example of the person returning from holiday again:

'What was the **food** like?'

'How was the **weather**?'

'When did you **leave**?'

'Where would you **stay** if you went back?'

'What kind of **activities** did they offer?'

We hope you can see that while these are still open questions, you are **leading** the other person to tell you about the thing that you want to hear about.

Tip: You can always think about what open neutral questions would be appropriate in advance of an event:

- *'What's your business?'/'How's business?'*
- *'Tell me about your family.'*
- *'What are your views on ...?'*
- *'What's your house like?'*
- *'What are your holiday plans this year?'*
- *'How would you describe ...?' (Basingstoke/Glasgow/Hampton in Arden/Hartlepool)*

If you can master the technique of asking great questions, you will be way ahead of most salespeople and could well end up raising your earning capacity by staggering amounts! And we're NOT joking. Our experience of working with thousands of salespeople over the past twenty years, is that very few of them are the masters of this particular art.

Do it yourself

Pick a subject area and think of as many open neutral and open leading questions as you can that you could ask when faced with this subject in any particular context.

Practise whenever and wherever you get the chance. Try this stuff out with colleagues at work, with friends and family, anywhere! The more you practise, the better you will get.

And, above all, get curious.

The more curious you become; the better questions you will ask. The better questions you ask, the more interesting you will become!

Keeping it going – speaking

So far we've concentrated on you listening and asking questions. The spotlight has been on the other person. Now it's time for us to turn the spotlight (how does that sound?) on you because at some point you're going to want to/have to contribute something of your own.

We explored some responses to typical questions you get asked in 'Starting points' earlier in the chapter. These responses add a bit more than the basic information and give the other person something to latch onto. In order to keep things going you can employ this technique at any time – even when you are asked a closed question!

> **Them:** 'Did you go to the office do?'
> **You:** 'I did and I thought it was brilliant. How about you?'

Them: 'Are you having a holiday this year?'
You: 'We are. We're off to Greece. I haven't been since I was a student.'

Here again you're giving the other person something to work with, but you're still handing over the baton pretty quickly.

In order to feel really confident about your ability to keep conversations going, whatever environment you walk into, planning is the key. As we said before, no actors go on stage without rehearsing, so why not take a leaf from their book?

Just imagine that you're going to a dinner party and you know that there will be some people there that you have never met before. Think for a minute about the kind of subjects that could come up in conversation:

- food
- holidays
- schools/education
- children
- local/national events
- sport
- work
- houses.

And there are probably more – and the list will change depending on the type of event you are attending.

Take one of these subjects and think through your own position. What do you feel about it? Do you have any particularly strong opinions about it? What experience do you have in that area? What would you like to know about it that you don't already know?

The idea is not to plan exactly what you might say but to get into a state whereby you are prepared to enter any of these conversation topics with confidence and a real belief that you have something to contribute.

And while you're at it you can consider what questions you could ask in order to discover what other people think about the subject.

"Remember: Being interested makes you interesting!"

If there are any areas where you feel you would like to know more; do some homework! If, for example, there is a big news story – airline staff are striking for Christmas! – and although you know about it, you really don't know the background to it, then get on the internet or pick up a paper and find out – and in the process pick up any other interesting or funny stories.

Not only does this mean that you will be able to contribute in a meaningful way if the subject comes up; it also means that you can raise the subject yourself and express an opinion about it at the same time. People love guests like you! You'll be invited back again.

Another great by-product is that you get to know a lot more about the world and enhance your own education. You also build up a repertoire of stories to tell.

Keeping it going – speaking up, speaking out

Have you ever been part of a conversation, wanted to make a contribution, not been quite sure what to say or when to say it and, just when you've worked that out, found that the conversation has moved on or ground to a halt and the moment is lost?

Have you ever wanted to put an idea forward, started to speak and found that you have been over-ridden by someone else, or not even been heard? Rest assured, these are pretty common occurrences.

*Tip: **Strike while the iron is hot!** The minute you feel that you want to say something, say it. Trust that your instinct is on your side and has chosen the very best moment for you to speak.*

Now that doesn't mean that you interrupt people, but it does mean that you pick the very best next moment to speak. How do you do that? Simply wait for the other person to pause as they take a breath or reach the end of a particular comment or story. And people take breaths at the end of sentences, so make sure you are listening. The rhythm of their speech and their content will tell you when this is coming.

One of the reasons that Margaret Thatcher was so difficult to interview was that she used to breathe in the middle of her sentences, so offering her interviewers very little opportunity to ask the next question!

Tip: When you do speak, come in with your point/start your story straight away.

Too often, we hear people start off in a way that is almost guaranteed to trigger an interruption:

> 'Er ... well ... I had quite an interesting thing happen to me a bit like that ... I mean it wasn't that interesting really, but, you know, it was very similar. Don't remember exactly when but ...'

If you want to get someone's attention you have to be positive and assertive both in speech and manner. So, the very least you need to do is make your opening statement one worth listening to.

> 'Your story reminds me of something that happened to us a couple of years ago. It was really very odd/funny/interesting, etc.'

Just look at what this sentence does:

- it shows you've been listening
- it shows you were interested in what they were saying
- it goes straight to the point
- it gives them a reason to carry on listening.

All you need to do is deliver it with confidence and you have a winning formula.

"Cut the waffle and HIT THE HEADLINE!"

So far we've been concentrating on setting you up to have a successful and enjoyable time at any event. Now let's look at some other strategies for interacting effectively with other people, regardless of the type of event you're attending. These strategies work anywhere at any time with anyone.

The unignorable handbag

Emma has an unignorable handbag. It is a thing of great beauty, of many colours and is totally **unignorable**. (We realise that word does not exist currently but we're making a case for it!) You know what we mean though. And, since it is fundamental to the successful implementation of this first strategy, we have named the strategy after it.

The question we have for you is: what is your 'unignorable handbag'? Before you answer that question, let's just clarify what the unignorable handbag is.

The unignorable handbag is something that you have which, when people see it for the first time, they feel compelled to ask about or comment on. And if you're a man reading this, don't think this doesn't apply to you.

You see, the thing about Emma's unignorable handbag is that people feel compelled to comment on it:

'Where did you get that wonderful bag?'

'What a great bag, where can I find one?'

'Wow, I've never seen a bag like that before.'

'Your bag is so unusual; may I look?'

Get the picture? What a great conversation starter.

So, your first task is to find your unignorable handbag and if you haven't got one, go and buy one!

For women this may be easier than for men, but it doesn't mean that men are excluded. For instance, Emma bought Tim a tie some time ago that usually excites some comment. He also has another quite interesting tie which Emma won't let him wear when he's with her, but which is guaranteed to cause a conversation. He has a very old – 60 years – gold wristwatch that his uncle gave him that is very dear to him and quite unusual when compared with the modern equivalent. And here's the thing. Even if the article itself doesn't cause comment, you can always draw people's attention to it.

The second part of this strategy is to be on the look-out for other people's unignorable handbags. These are the things that they are wearing or carrying that quite obviously mean something to them or over which they have spent time or which they have chosen with care. These things then become great conversation openers. Simply follow the formulas above:

'Where did you get that **beautiful** ...?'

'What a **terrific** ...'

'I **love** that ... you're wearing.'

And wherever you can, take the opportunity to add a complimentary word or phrase into your question or comment, as we've highlighted above.

All of which brings us onto the subject of compliments; how and when to give them.

Compliments that win; compliments that don't

As with so many things, there is an art to giving compliments. That doesn't mean it's difficult to do; it just means you need to think before you deliver.

So take a moment or two to think about the compliments that you have been paid.

- Which are the ones you remember best?
- Which ones mean most to you?
- Who gave them to you?
- How did they give them?
- How did you feel about it when they gave them?

Ideally, this exercise should be a very positive experience for you. You should remember those compliments fondly as well as the person or people who gave them to you.

Tim remembers only too well one of our great friends saying to him: 'Tim, what I love about you is the way you always make me feel so special.' He treasures that more, yes, even more, than his 60-year-old watch!

And this of course is what we all want to achieve when we give anyone a compliment. It's also important to take into account any other people who may be in earshot when we give the compliment. Why? Because a compliment given to one person may contain unconscious criticism of another.

So, here are some rules for giving compliments that really hit the spot.

Only give compliments when you REALLY mean it. People who throw compliments around like confetti devalue the compliment and can easily be regarded as being at best insincere and at worst 'brown nosing'!

Give compliments that are specific and not generalised – 'You're great' isn't half as effective as the ones below – so that the person can see that you have taken the trouble to 'design' the compliment to fit the circumstances:

> 'That was a fabulous party, you are so good at getting people who hardly know each other to have a great time.'

> 'You have an amazing ability to make people feel that they are the only person in the room.'

Give compliments that reinforce whatever the person does/has done that you like:

'You always look so attractive; you're a model for us all.'

'I just don't know how you manage to achieve so much and still have time for your friends. Whatever it is, please keep doing it.'

When you do give compliments, think about the best time and place to give them. Often this will be in a quiet moment with the person concerned and no one else present. Make sure you have good eye contact so that they can see that you mean it. Make it a special occasion.

When you want to compliment someone in public, make sure that you are not accidentally upsetting anyone else. To compliment someone who is so much slimmer as a result of taking up exercise when there are others present who know that they need to lose weight is not the best recipe for lasting relationships!

Sometimes you can abandon all those rules and, when the moment takes you, just offer a one or two word compliment that adds spring to the other person's step:

'Great meal.'

'You look terrific.'

'What a party.'

'Good speech.'

Whatever you do, remember above all; MEAN IT and BELIEVE IT!

Turning small talk to big talk – getting 'below the waterline'

Most of what we've covered so far in this chapter has been to do with 'small talk'. That's a common phrase but what do we mean by it?

Let's think of it in relation to an iceberg. The principle of the iceberg is that approximately 10 per cent of its mass is above the waterline and 90 per cent below. In terms of conversations, most conversations between strangers take place 'above the waterline'.

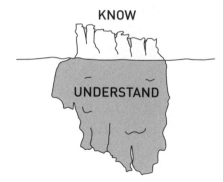

In other words they communicate at a surface level and share information that is comfortable for them to share and that does not expose them in the early days of a relationship.

At this level we talk about where we live; what we do; who our family consists of; what our hobbies are; where we went for our holidays; in other words, 'small talk'.

By and large this is information that we are happy to exchange with others and it is the fuel for most conversations. It is having the information that lies at this level that allows us to say we **know** someone.

We all know that it's different with friends and people who we have known for a long time. We operate at a deeper level – 'below the waterline'. At this level we talk about **understanding** someone; about being on the same wavelength; about sharing the same values; about being close.

We have often thought that it isn't by chance that the word, 'UNDERSTAND', begins with 'UNDER'. The idea being that we have to, metaphorically speaking, don our scuba diving gear and go diving below the surface of what is obvious to find the real pearls.

You'll no doubt have heard the phrase, 'once you get to know them'. We prefer to think of this as, 'once you get to understand them'. Now we're in the realms of 'big talk'.

So why would we want to move from 'small talk' to 'big talk'?

Well, if your experience is anything like ours, then you have found that there are some people with whom, although you have only just met, you feel an instant sense of rapport; you really do see things the same way, are on the same wavelength, feel like you've known them for ages.

And when you find this, then you have a great chance to capitalise on it and begin to form what may become a long and enjoyable friendship.

The question is how do you start the process without looking over-enthusiastic, bombarding them with signals that say, 'I want to be your friend' and perhaps turning them off?

Well, actually, it's very easy and here are a couple of great strategies for getting 'below the waterline' in a way that keeps you in rapport and also displays your interest in knowing more.

Diving for opinions

If we continue to use the iceberg and scuba diving ideas, then think of the 'above the waterline' information as facts and see these as offering you a springboard that allows you to jump off to explore what lies beneath them. The best way to use the springboard? Ask a question. And, remembering what Krishnamurti said, the question you ask is aimed at discovering what lies beneath the fact.

Let's look at some examples:

Someone volunteers the information that their child goes to a private school.
'What's your view/opinion/what do you think of private education?'

'We go to Greece every year for our holidays.'
'What is it about Greece that attracts you?'

'We moved here from Scotland a couple of years ago.'
'And how do you feel about the move now?'

'I'd never go self-employed.'
'What would stop you?'

You will see that all these questions are asking the speaker to offer not only more information but also to give you an insight into their thinking and their opinions about the various subjects. Whilst this doesn't necessarily get you very far below the waterline, it's going to give you a whole lot more to explore.

If you want to go much deeper then try the next strategy.

Diving for values

For anyone who wants to develop a really deep level of understanding of another person and who is keen to build a more meaningful relationship with them, this strategy can deliver the treasure at the bottom of the sea!

But before we give you the strategy, it's worth spending a few moments considering why diving for values is such a rewarding thing to do.

And the place to start is with a brief explanation of what values are.

Values represent what is important to us; variety, achievement, integrity, honesty, openness, recognition, happiness, freedom. They are one of the most influential of the filters that we talked about in Chapter 1.

We can often hold a value and not know it until it is not being met. We might not consciously consider 'variety' to be important to us until we find ourselves in a situation which restricts our internal definition of what variety means to us. Then we can become dissatisfied. It is often easier to know when we are not getting a value met than when we are.

Values can be context-specific, so that we can have different values for different parts of our lives – relationships, work, family, etc. They are the unconscious yardsticks which inform our decision making and also provide us with our method for evaluating decisions once they have been made.

Consider yourself for a moment. The reason you are reading this book is that being able to talk to anyone in every situation is important to you. If it wasn't, you wouldn't have bought it. If you are interested to know what values you have that led you to make the decision to buy, then here's an exercise for you:

Exercise

What's important?

Take a few minutes to jot down the answer to this question:

'What's important to you about being able to talk to anyone with confidence?'

What did you discover? Were there any surprises or did you know that all the time?

Whatever your response, we'll take a guess at one thing. Not too many people in your life would know your answers to that question. And would it be true to say that anyone who did know your answers would be pretty close to you? Would they be someone who you trust or would you want to share that information with just anyone?

If we're anywhere near the truth, then you can see how understanding a person's values brings you very close to them, can't you? So it makes sense that, if you in turn want to get closer to someone else, you focus your energies on getting to understand their values.

And, as there's really only one question that you need to ask, this is not only a very powerful strategy, it's also an easy one to implement.

Here's the question: **'What's important to you about ...?'**

You can use this question, or a form of it, in any environment, in relation to any particular issue that you want to explore. For example:

Them: 'I go to the gym every day.'
You: 'What's important to you about going to the gym?'

Them: 'I love my job; I get to meet a lot of different people.'
You: 'And what is it you love about meeting different people?'

Asking this question gives you not only the person's values in relation to the topic but also offers you a great opportunity to explore these values in more detail, so building an even deeper level of rapport. For example:

Them: 'I go to the gym every day.'

You: 'What's important to you about going to the gym?'

Them: 'It keeps me fit and active.'

You: 'Fit and active for what?'

Them: 'Well, I want to make sure I'm still around when the kids are grown up.'

So now you have discovered that what is REALLY important to them about going to the gym is their fitness in relation to their children. A hugely important by-product of this strategy is that it avoids us making assumptions about other people's values and reasons for doing things. I wonder whether your answer to the question 'What's important to you about going to the gym?' (if, of course, you go to the gym) would be the same?

Toe-curlers and vote winners

Of course, sometimes things don't quite go according to plan. Have you ever had an 'awkward moment'? They are those toe-curling moments when:

- you run out of things to say and so does the person you are talking to
- you find yourself babbling on and realise you are talking nonsense
- you make an inappropriate comment
- you raise a topic and suddenly realise it was NOT a good idea
- you want to get away from someone but feel completely stuck.

Let's have a look at some ways of turning toe-curlers into vote winners.

You run out of things to say and so do they

This is perhaps one of the most common toe-curlers, particularly when you are meeting someone for the first time. At a party it's not quite such an issue but if it's your first date ... and silence reigns!

So what do confident people do? Well, one thing that marks out confident people in this situation is that they are comfortable with silence. You see, it all depends on how you think about silence. For most of us it tends to signal the onrush of feelings of panic. We start to search feverishly for something to say. We think that it is our responsibility to break the silence and then start worrying about what the other person must be thinking. So our search for something to say becomes ever more desperate and the more we search, the less we find.

For the confident person it signals a pause in proceedings and the fact that they remain relaxed means that, more often than not, they find something to say and the conversation starts all over again.

Now, becoming comfortable with silence could be a step too far at this stage, so what can the rest of us do until we become that confident? Well, we can use some of the techniques we've discussed already. But before you do anything, take a nice, deep breath and relax:

Use the 'unignorable handbag' or equivalent, e.g.:

'I've been admiring that ring/watch/jacket, etc. you're wearing. Where did you get it?'

'This is a great house for a party; we could never get all this lot into our place. How about you?'

'What a great spread they've put on. What's your favourite food?'

'I wonder where they got that sofa/table/wallpaper/picture, etc, from. Where do you go shopping for your furniture/...../...../etc?'

Pick up on something you have already talked about and find out more:

'You know you were telling me earlier about your dogs. What advice would you give to someone who wanted to get a dog but who had a very small child?'

'I know you're going to Greece for your holidays this year, but where would you go if you could just jet off for the whole of the summer?'

Dig into the bag of information that you've brought with you – your life, what you've read in the papers, etc:

'This party reminds me of one I went to when I lived in Birmingham. How well do you know the Midlands?'

'Have you heard about the airline strikes they're predicting for the summer? What are your holiday plans?'

You find yourself babbling on and realise you are talking nonsense

Our favourite way of handling this situation (because it works really well and Emma should know, given the number of times she has to use it!) is: 'Oh, good heavens, listen to me babbling away. Right, I'll stop!' (said with a self-deprecating smile). This is great because not only does it get a 'Don't be silly, of course you're not' response – even though you are – it also:

● shows you are human

● shows you are self-aware

● shows you are aware of others

● helps to build rapport – just think how many other people will have babbled on at some stage

● makes you stop!

You make an inappropriate comment/raise a topic and suddenly realise it was NOT a good idea

Gary's story

(names changed to protect the innocent)

Gary was at a party held to bring together ex-pupils of his old school. He bumps into an old classmate, Charlie, and the conversation goes as follows:

Gary: Charlie! Great to see you again. How are things?

Charlie: Really good. How about you?

Gary: Yeah, fine . . .

At this point Gary spies Sally on the other side of the room. Sally was in the same class as he and Charlie.

Gary: Oh God, there's Sally. Prepare to be bored. Remember her?

Charlie: Yes, we got married last year.

The first thing, of course, is to recognise that you've made an inappropriate comment. You've probably met people who seem quite oblivious to the fact that they've put their foot in something and carry on regardless, while all around them the new Ice Age is forming!

If you recognise what you've done, you're more than halfway towards a great resolution. And let's be clear about something here. This kind of situation is embarrassing for everyone, regardless of how confident they are.

So how do you recognise what you've done? What are the signals that tell you you're on ground that you should keep clear of?

In Chapter 4 we're going to give you some terrific ways of building rapport and a wealth of information about the ways in which you can notice changes in people's thinking and behaviour. Also, in Chapter 6, we're going to give you some really effective ways of handling difficult situations, so at this stage we'll cover the basic elements.

We've already talked earlier in this chapter about keeping your focus on the person you're talking to; in being **interested**. If you do this, then you'll notice when anything changes. So you'll **see** the changes, in their facial expression, physiology and state – have a look at Chapter 2 if you want to recap. You may well **hear** the changes in the tone of their voice and you may also get a **feeling** that something has changed. Have you ever had that experience of just **knowing** you've said something you shouldn't have said?

Now you've got three options:

- carry on and ignore it
- change the subject
- acknowledge what's happened and move on.

Which to choose? Well, actually, in our view there's only one route to take and that's the **own up to it** route. Say something along the lines of:

'Oh, I'm so sorry. Me and my big mouth!'

'I can't believe I said that. I'm really sorry.'

And then **shut up**!

The same strategy holds good if you raise a topic that you suddenly realise was **not** a good idea. Simply acknowledge the fact and hand over to someone else or, if there are only two of you, steer off in a different direction or ask a question.

'I'm sorry, I can see that you would rather not talk about it. How about we have another coffee?'

'I hope you'll forgive me for raising the issue. Let's change the subject. What have you got planned for the rest of the week?'

What you'll notice with all these strategies is that they give you the chance to extricate yourself as well as leaving an impression of someone who cares about the other person/people and is aware of the impact they have. These are **good** messages to leave behind you.

If you want to encapsulate all that advice into one sentence:

"When you're in a hole, stop digging!"

You want to get away but feel completely stuck

We've all had moments when we've found ourselves talking to someone and wishing we could stop the conversation and move on.

Sometimes they're people who have no idea of the impact they're having on others and just ramble on regardless. They believe that what they're saying is endlessly fascinating and that you are pretty lucky to be there.

Sometimes they are shy, nervous people whose nervousness finds its expression in almost incessant talking.

And one of the main reasons for us getting stuck with them is because we don't want to upset or offend them, even if they are doing their best to qualify for the 'Bore of Britain' award.

So, our aim is to break contact while making them feel OK about it. We want to do it nicely, so here's our **NICE** approach:

N: Name – We all respond to our name. We can't not respond. We're programmed to respond. So if you want to stop someone in their tracks, the very best way to do this is to use their name. Now you have their attention.

I: Interest – Tell them that you have been interested in what they have been saying. Express pleasure in having been talking to them. In other words, make them feel good about themselves.

C: Conclude – Conclude the conversation by explaining what you intend to do next.

E: Exit – Exit pleasantly giving them the assurance that you are looking forward to catching up with them again in the future.

Let's put it all together:

N: 'George, it's been lovely talking to you and it was good to hear about your kids.

I: They sound like a smashing couple of boys.

C: I really want to see if I can find Mary before she goes, so please forgive me if I nip off now.

E: I hope we get the chance to catch up again soon.'

The language we use may not work for you and if it doesn't simply do it in your own fashion. Whatever feels most comfortable for you will be the thing that works the best. Just follow the **NICE** formula.

Tip: If you want to feel really confident using the formula, practise it until it becomes second nature.

Chapter

4

How to build rapport and connect with anyone

Have you ever had the experience of being with someone you get on with and suddenly noticing that you were doing the same things? You were taking a drink at the same time; you were walking down the road in step; you were laughing at the same moment; you were sitting in an almost identical position; you scratched your head and they scratched theirs. It happens all the time and for the overwhelming majority of that time we are not consciously aware of it. All we know is that being with that other person is pretty easy and enjoyable. That's rapport.

There are some people with whom you feel, from the first moment of meeting, a natural affinity and there are others whose immediate impact on you is less positive. And this is the way of the world.

The interesting thing is that we can come to decisions about people in a moment. You've probably had the same experience that we have. You've walked into a room, at a party perhaps, and there have been people there that you have never met. You've scanned the room and generally speaking the women amongst us are a lot better at that than the men, but that's a subject for another time. Someone has caught your eye and without a moment's hesitation you find yourself thinking, 'They look nice; I'd like to have a chat to them later.'

Equally, you'll have seen someone else and for no apparent reason find yourself thinking, 'I don't think so!'

So what's going on? How does that work?

Just think for a moment about the first time you met a particular person. Maybe you've been somewhere recently where you were introduced to someone you had never met before. If so, try and recall that moment.

- What did you notice about them?
- What was your first impression?
- What judgements did you make?

Whether we like it or not, we make judgements about people pretty quickly. And we make judgements based on a whole set of criteria.

Now, if it's me you're judging, there are certain things I can do nothing about and there are others that I can do something about. I can do nothing about my height, my age, my sex, my ethnicity, my accent (unless I train to get rid of it).

I can, however, do something about my appearance, my dress, my hair, my scent, my eye contact, my handshake, my posture, my gestures, my facial expression, my tone of voice, the words I use in greeting.

It's important to recognise what people pay attention to in the first moments of meeting so that we can ensure we create a really positive first impression. You'll no doubt have heard the phrase, 'You never have a second chance to make a good first impression', and it's amazing how much weight we give to those first moments.

That's not to say that a less than positive first impression cannot be reversed but it takes a good deal of time and contrary evidence to do it. In which case it makes enormous sense to do whatever we can to ensure that people's first experience of us is a good one.

So what do we pay attention to in those first moments?

When you think about the lists of things we notice, both those you can do something about and those you cannot, you'll see that they split into three main areas:

- **Verbal**: the words that I use.
- **Vocal**: the tone of my voice, speed, rhythm, volume, etc.
- **Visual**: my appearance, posture, gestures, facial expressions.

So what you witness is a kind of 'bundle' of communication.

Now the question arises; which of these do we pay most attention to? For the answer to that question, we'll go to the work of Albert Mehrabian, who studied the relative importance of these three areas in the first moments of meeting and their impact on the degree to which we make a 'like/dislike' judgement of the person concerned. He then converted this information into percentage scores for each area.

We appreciate that for some of you this may be familiar territory but for those who have never seen this before, why not take a guess before you look at the results and see how closely your experience matches that of Mehrabian.

The results he arrived at were quite surprising. The relative importance we attach, in percentage terms, to each of these three areas is:

- verbal: 7 per cent
- vocal: 38 per cent
- visual: 55 per cent.

What does this all mean? Firstly, we should point out what it doesn't mean. It doesn't mean that our words are not important. Of course they're important. What it does mean is that in terms of making a 'like'/'dislike' judgement in the very early stages of meeting, we pay an enormous amount of attention to what we see. And you'll probably have loads of examples of times you've made a judgement about someone before they've even spoken to you.

The other thing worth noting here is that the visual and vocal messages are received at an unconscious level while the verbal signals (words) are processed at a conscious level.

The reason for pointing this out is to ensure that you understand the importance of the first two on the basis that our reactions to them are completely spontaneous. We see someone; we make a judgement. We don't look at them, pause and think to ourselves: 'Now, let's see. Their tie is not quite done up. They appear not to have combed the left side of their hair. I notice that their shoulders are slightly hunched as if they were somewhat intimidated. And they're not looking directly into my eyes; indeed they seem to be addressing a point almost 2.5 inches above my left eyebrow. On the basis of the information gleaned, I have decided that I will not trust them.'

It doesn't work like that. It works in a split second as the image in front of us flies through our filtering system, raiding our internal computer for every relevant example and coming up with a response in less time than it takes to blink an eye.

And in that 'blink of an eye', what are we searching for? You'll have no doubt heard the phrase, 'people like people like them'. And you know the truth of that. Look around any group of friends or colleagues that get on particularly well and you'll soon be able to pick out the things they have in common. We are always, unconsciously, on the look-out for people like us.

And of course we tend to choose to spend the majority of our time with the people we get on with best. What a surprise! And with these people rapport occurs naturally. We really don't have to think about it.

But what happens when we meet people with whom we find it more difficult to communicate? We've all experienced it at one time or another. You meet someone who you need to be able to get on with and find them quite difficult to connect with. This is when the skill of building rapport comes into its own. And it's one of the skills that all confident conversationalists display.

Whatever your particular reasons for reading this book; whatever situations you find most challenging, whether at work or in your personal and social life; whoever you want to be able to talk to confidently, you will achieve your aims with greater success and ease once you master the skills of rapport building.

They are skills that are essential for relationship building, for creating trust, for enabling us to change the nature of our less than positive experiences and for developing deeper levels of understanding.

And, rest assured, they are **skills** and that means that you can learn them. Sure, it may take time to master them but the effort will be well worth it. Why? Because rapport is the essence of all successful communication; the ultimate tool for producing results with other people.

You're a lot like me

We've already talked about how we filter our moment-by-moment experiences on the basis of our beliefs, values and experiences, so it comes as no surprise to realise that when we meet people for the first time we apply these filters. And given that we've already agreed that we are looking for people like us, we filter for similarity.

In other words we are searching for any signal that indicates that a partnership could be formed. And those indicators will include:

- physical appearance
- posture
- gesture and movement
- voice tone
- language
- beliefs
- values.

Given what we have already said about the work of Mehrabian (7 per cent verbal; 38 per cent vocal; 55 per cent visual), we will be particularly influenced in the very first moments by the first four elements on our list. These are the elements whose instant impact we process unconsciously. So at this point it's worth reinforcing this:

"We cannot, not communicate."

We can be as quiet and unobtrusive as possible; we can think we are having no impact at all; we can even decide that we want to be, to all intents and purposes, invisible. Will other people notice, will they make judgements about us? They certainly will.

Have you ever been to a 'do' of any sort and felt like being quiet? Maybe you didn't know too many people. Maybe you were just enjoying it and wanted to listen and not talk. And then someone comes up to you and says, 'You're being very quiet tonight, are you all right?'

The point is that people are constantly making judgements about us, about the state we're in. And we're doing the same to them!

How can we use this information to enable us to build rapport quickly and easily so that we can talk with confidence? Indeed, how can we use this information to smooth our path into the first conversation, given that that is usually the most challenging one? Have you ever found that once the ice has been broken, things flow more smoothly?

Well, the first thing to do is to ensure that we are in the best possible state – a state of confidence – the moment we walk in the door.

So what can we do, in those very first moments, to make a connection and to convey the message of confidence? Well, think about the confident people that you know. Do they slouch? Do they look at the ground? Do they avoid eye contact? Absolutely not. Why not? Because the way we hold ourselves, our physiology, has an enormous impact on how we feel; the state we're in. If you go around looking down at the ground all the time, you'll soon find yourself feeling 'down'. Conversely, it's well nigh impossible to feel 'down' if you keep looking 'up'.

What you will find is that whenever you feel nervous or anxious, you will have a certain physiology attached to that state. You'll hold yourself in a certain way; look in certain directions; use certain gestures; have a particular tone to your voice.

Tip: If you want to change your state, change your physiology.

If you want not only to feel confident but also to exude confidence, take on the physiology of confidence:

- Stand up straight.
- Keep your head erect.
- Make good, direct eye contact making sure that you:
  - keep contact long enough for it to register as meaningful, but not so long that it intimidates
  - notice how much eye contact your companions are comfortable with and adapt accordingly (the more you focus on others, the less likely you will be to feel nervous)
  - make sure you make eye contact with everyone in the group you are talking to
  - smile! – never underestimate the impact and power of a genuine smile; on you and others.
- Adopt and maintain an assertive stance:
  - stand with your feet hip width apart (this works for both men and women)
  - keep your weight evenly balanced.
- When walking, walk with purpose.
- Breathe deeply and easily. Breathing deeply – from your diaphragm as opposed to your upper chest – sends a signal to the brain that you are relaxed and confident. If you have ever found yourself being attacked by nerves and need to do something in the moment to put them to one side, we have some more great strategies for you in Chapter 7.

Tip: If you want to pick the ONE attribute from this list that will have the most impact and convey confidence more emphatically than any other it's EYE CONTACT. We attach more importance to eye contact as evidence of confidence than we do to anything else.

And eye contact is the easiest way for us to connect with another person. It's the beginning of everything as far as a relationship of any sort is concerned and the main key to rapport.

So, if you really want to be able to talk to anyone in any situation and do it with confidence, start by developing your ability to make good, direct eye contact.

Exercise

Changing states

1. Practise getting into a confident state by changing your physiology. Work out for yourself the physiology that works best for you and keep practising it.

2. The next time you go anywhere to meet anyone, concentrate on making great eye contact and notice what a positive difference it makes.

Now that we've given you the strategies to get into a positive, confident state, let's consider for a moment what happens when people are in rapport. How do we know they are in rapport?

If you look at people in bars, restaurants and wherever you do your people-watching, you could probably tell intuitively which groups are friends and which are not. If you observe carefully you may notice different patterns of behaviour which groups exhibit. Friends – those groups in good rapport – will be engaged in something resembling a dance of mutual-responsiveness. The movements of one person will be echoed or mirrored by another or others in the group. For example, if one person leans forward, the person they are talking to may also lean forward or shift their posture in that direction.

Watch two people who are in rapport and you will notice that their posture, gestures, patterns and rhythms of speech are similar. If they are walking down the street together you may notice that they walk in step.

"She stopped and leant her elbows against the parapet of the embankment. He did likewise. There is at times a magic in identity of position; it is one of the things that have suggested to us eternal comradeship.**"** E.M. Forster, *A Room with a View*, 1908

All of these people are **'matching'** each other. This occurs naturally at an unconscious level. Almost always, when we are working in this area in the workshops we run, participants will 'fall into rapport' and will be completely unaware of the ways in which they are matching each other until we point it out to them. And that in an environment where rapport is the subject of intense scrutiny! So in the surroundings of normal life, people are rarely, if ever, consciously aware of what is going on.

And if you've ever been in rapport with anyone, you'll know the positive effects that it can have:

- you enjoy their company
- you feel you can talk to them
- you see things the same way
- you are on the same wavelength
- you feel close to them
- you look forward to seeing them.

All of which means, that the skills of rapport building can have a truly magical effect on your relationships. And the great thing is, they **are** skills and they **can** be learned.

First things first

Before we start looking at how to build rapport, it's important to get some foundations in place. If you're going to be successful in building rapport and forming good relationships with people, you have to want to do it! If you really aren't interested in and curious about the people you're with, it's going to show.

You'll probably have met people at one time or another who **appear** to be interested in you but your experience is very different. You just know they're not. Sometimes it's obvious – they keep looking over your shoulder at other people while you're talking to them – and sometimes it's just a gut feeling you get that tells you, 'They couldn't really care less!' Everything they do feels false. And the reason it feels false is because it **is** false and you can't get away with false. So, take everything we give you in this chapter, in this whole book in fact, and use it with integrity, with commitment and with a positive intention to discover more about the people you meet and it will work brilliantly for you.

So, take a pause here and decide what you really want. Because if you do REALLY want to be able to talk to anyone in any situation with confidence AND leave behind you a trail of goodwill, you need to commit to being interested and curious.

Of course, you're going to come up against people that you don't necessarily like; you're going to find yourself in situations that are more challenging; you're sometimes going to want to NOT have certain conversations:

- with a manager you don't get on with
- with a colleague who drives you up the wall
- with a professional who tries to blind you with science
- with someone you find particularly overbearing
- when you have to make a complaint
- when you have to stand up for yourself
- when you have to tell a friend that they've done something that's upset you.

The fact of the matter is, though, that if you go into these conversations with a real **desire** to understand, to put your point across in an effective and assertive way, and to build whatever level of rapport you can that will help you achieve your outcome, you will become way more successful in your relationships.

So, before you think of immersing yourself in the skills of building rapport, just ensure that whatever conversation you enter, you do it from a standpoint of wanting to establish areas of mutual interest.

With the people you like, it's easy. You already have areas of mutual interest otherwise you probably wouldn't be friends. So that's the first thing to consider with those people you like less. What can you do to establish what those areas might be?

Well, the first thing is to find out and that's what you do with the questions that we explored in Chapter 3. But, **and this is really important,** you need to have some level of rapport before you start asking questions. It makes sense, doesn't it? You wouldn't be too happy if someone you didn't know just walked straight up to you and started firing questions at you.

And that's what we're going to do now. We're going to give you the easiest, fastest ways of building rapport, that then give you the opportunity to ask the questions you want to ask to start the ball rolling.

Building rapport – planning rapport

You may well have heard the phrase, 'If you fail to plan, you plan to fail'. We don't want you to get robotic and incredibly businesslike about things; we want you to really enjoy the conversations you have and the events you go to. We do, however, think that preparation and planning, particularly in the early days of learning and implementing the strategies in this book, can be very useful. In time, it becomes second nature.

So what has planning to do with building rapport?

Well, if you find yourself being invited to an event where you are going to meet people from a particular industry; people who have a particular pastime – you're invited to the sailing club/tennis club/darts club/golf club/football club/rugby club (you can probably think of loads more) annual party; people who work for a local charity; people who support a local cause, then it pays to prepare:

- Do some background research – club history/current season's results, etc.
- Find out about the sport/pastime.
- Learn some of the terminology – birdies/mainsails/penalty shoot-outs/double tops can be interesting!
- Get some questions ready – you don't need to know everything, so you can make a virtue of your relative ignorance by showing you're interested in finding out more.

There's nothing that helps build rapport more quickly and easily than your demonstration of interest and the fact that you've bothered to find out something before you turned up. Besides anything else, at least it gives you an outside chance of understanding what they're talking about!

Building rapport – learning the dance

In the next part of this chapter we're going to outline the various aspects of behaviour that we employ to build rapport with another person and then introduce you to the techniques and strategies that you can use to help you to build rapport with anyone you want to. Yes, even the 'difficult' ones!

There's a lot here and we know that sometimes the whole thing can seem a bit overwhelming. We've had people say to us, 'Oh, it's all very well for you but how on earth am I supposed to take in all this information? There's just too much to do!'

Well, here's the good news. You don't have to take it all in. In fact, we'd suggest you don't even try to take it all in. What you need to do is adopt the 'eat the elephant' approach. Take it in small bites! And here's how to do that.

> **Bite 1**: Start to notice what people do who are in rapport. Sit in a café, a pub, a restaurant, sit on a bench in a park; anywhere that people gather. And then all you need to do is to watch. And, if it helps, take some notes. Do whatever works best for you so that you get to be really familiar with recognising rapport.
>
> You'll also start to notice, of course, what happens when people are NOT in rapport.

> **Bite 2**: Bring it closer to home. Start noticing what happens when you're with friends and acquaintances or work colleagues. Begin to become even more aware of how people operate. And you can also begin to notice how you are responding.
>
> Notice the differences between your behaviour when you are with people you like and those who you find a bit more of a challenge.

We'll give you a couple more 'bites' after the next section.

Matching

The primary skill of rapport building is that of **matching** and the first element of the skill is the ability to pay close attention – remember the Chinese symbol for listening – to the following:

- posture
- gesture and movement
- voice tone
- language
- breathing.

Once you've got your attention focused on how someone is communicating, the next step, if you want to get into rapport with them, is to start **matching** what they are doing. And so now we're going to go through these areas one by one and look at what we can do to match someone and also give you some **tips** that will help you do this really well and really easily.

Let's imagine we're meeting someone for the first time. We walk into the room and what do we notice?

Posture:

- Are they sitting or standing?
- How do they hold themselves? Do they hold themselves erect? Do they slouch? Do they face you straight on? Do they turn slightly away from you?
- How do they distribute their weight? Do they distribute it evenly? Do they stand with more weight on one foot than another? Do they stand still or shift their weight around?
- If sitting, are their legs crossed or uncrossed? Are they leaning back in the chair or forward? Arms folded or unfolded?
- Do they put their head to one side? Do they hold it straight?

Gesture, movement and facial expression:

- How do they move? Do they move with deliberation/slowly? Or do they move more quickly/spontaneously?

- Do they use a lot of gestures or very few? Are their gestures kept fairly close to their body or do they gesture expansively? What kind of rhythm do they use to gesture; flowing or staccato?

- Do they use their hands a lot? Do they keep them clasped or closed? Do they fidget?

- Are they smiling or frowning?

- Are they making direct eye contact or looking away?

- Do they tend to focus on you or on other parts of the room/ space?

Voice tone:

- Pace: fast or slow?

- Pitch: high or low?

- Tone: monotone or varied?

- Rhythm: varied or even?

- Volume: loud or soft?

- Pauses: few or many?

Language:

- What kind of language do they use: Visual, Auditory, Kinaesthetic? (We're going to do more on this in a minute.)

Breathing:

- Rate: fast or slow?

- Depth: shallow or deep?

Now this is where you may be thinking, 'That's a hell of a lot to be paying attention to!' and you'd be right. But actually that's exactly what you are paying attention to all the time; you're just not consciously aware that you're doing it.

So now it's time for:

> **Bite 3:** The next time you're going somewhere and you know that you're going to be meeting new people, choose just **one area** to focus on. So off you go, saying to yourself, 'Tonight I'm looking at gestures and I'm not going to bother about

anything else.' And then the next time, it's tone of voice and so on.

Very soon you'll find that you're picking up an amazing amount of information without having to think about it.

The best place to start, of course, is with the people you know and get on with. Simply start to notice how they operate. And have a great time doing it.

What to do with it once you've got it

So, now you're getting pretty good at noticing what's going on, what do you do with the information? **You use it.** You use it to build rapport. You start **matching** the person you're with. In other words, you start to do some of the things that they do – stand in the same way, speak with the same rhythm, use the same kinds of gestures, so that they perceive you to be like them.

Bite 4: Pick **ONE** thing to match – posture, gesture, vocal tone, etc. and the next time you're with someone, start to notice how they operate in that particular area and begin to match them.

Every single one of the areas we have outlined above gives you an opportunity for matching. Let's run through some examples so that you can see how this will work:

- **Posture** ... Assume for a moment that the person you want to build rapport with is sitting down, leaning back in their chair with their legs crossed. You come in, sit down and then adopt the same position. You are now matching.

- **Voice** ... Let's say that you have a fairly loud voice and speak quickly without many pauses. The person you meet has a tendency to speak quite quietly, slowly and pauses frequently. You adjust your speech patterns to theirs and speak more quietly. You are now matching.

So far, so good, but what happens when they change position? You follow and change your position BUT, **and please pay**

close attention to this, you don't do it immediately because it will soon become very obvious what you are doing!

You leave it a few seconds and then make the adjustments necessary.

If we apply matching to our examples above, then this is what you would do:

- **Posture** ... They move and uncross their legs. To stay in rapport, you wait a moment or two and then uncross yours.
- **Voice** ... They become very enthused about an issue you are discussing and start to speak more quickly and a little more loudly. As you respond to them, you raise the volume of your voice and speed up your rate of speech.

These are some of the basic strategies associated with matching. We're going to come back to these later in the book, when we address the issues of talking with confidence to people in difficult situations; when they are being aggressive, angry, or indeed, shy and withdrawn.

> **Bite 5**: Try matching a number of different people, picking only **one** behaviour each time, and notice what happens and how successful you are.

> **Bite 6**: Try matching **more than one** behaviour.
> By doing it in small chunks, you'll soon find that you are combining the different matching opportunities without really having to think about it. It will soon be 'in the muscle'.

"Remember that matching is a **SKILL** and if you're going to get good at it, you have to **PRACTISE**."

Matching in language (1)

You'll remember that when we introduced the 'process of communication' in Chapter 2, we talked about our thoughts being coded in Visual, Auditory and Kinaesthetic forms. Well, most people have a preference. Most of us have a preferred form for storing information.

As a result of our preference for storing that information, we will tend to use that form or language pattern when we then share that information. So you will hear people use words that demonstrate their preferred way of thinking. For example:

Visual:

'I **see** what you mean.'

'**Looks** good to me.'

'I get the **picture**.'

Auditory:

'That **sounds** like a good idea.'

'I **hear** what you're saying.'

'We're on the same **wavelength**.'

Kinaesthetic:

'It **feels** like the right thing to do.'

'We're going to take the **rough with the smooth**.'

'What does your **instinct** tell you to do?'

Now what does this mean and what are the implications for rapport?

Well, it means that if Mr Visual meets Ms Kinaesthetic they are quite likely to find that they are, almost literally, 'speaking a different language'.

Can you see now how some people find it difficult to build rapport when they are operating in different forms? If you have ever heard someone say something along these lines:

'They just don't **see** it the way I do.'

or

'We're **out of tune** with each other.'

or

'We don't **feel** the same way about things.'

you've probably been listening to a clash of language patterns; people thinking in different ways and wondering why they don't get on.

If you want to become a really excellent communicator and have the confidence that you are really speaking 'their language', then listen out for the way in which the other person is talking – which language pattern they are using – and use it in return. For example:

Them: 'I **see** there's a new restaurant in town.'
You: 'Yes, I **noticed** it the other day. I like the **look** of the menu.'

Them: 'I **hear** they've decided to go to Greece this year.'
You: '**Sounds** like a good idea to me.'

Them: 'I really **feel** for the Smith's. They've had to **put up with** all that building work.'
You: 'It must be **annoying**. I think they've **held up** pretty well.'

If you want to check out your own preference then think about the last holiday you had and imagine you were describing it to a friend. How would you describe it? Would you:

- Tell them about the scenery, the colours, the blue of the sky, how white the snow was? (Visual)

- Tell them about the sound of the sea, the silence around you, the music you heard, the sound of the skis over the snow? (Auditory)

- Tell them about how relaxing it was, the heat of the sun, the warmth of the water, the feel of the snow under your skis, the rush of the wind in your face? (Kinaesthetic)

The fact is, that people will switch from one to another during the course of a conversation, so keep your focus of attention on them, keep listening and, if you're with someone you haven't met before, match their preferred pattern – at least for the first few moments of your time together. This will allow you to build a good level of rapport and once you have done that, the matching of your language will become less important.

Here are some of the words to listen out for that will signal the different ways of thinking:

Visual	Auditory	Kinaesthetic
Clear	Listen	Touch
Dim	Hear	Feel
Foggy	Tune	Grasp
Hazy	Remark	Handle
View	Pronounce	Pressure
Focus	Enquire	Cling
Picture	Voice	Numb
Clarify	Chatter	Soft
Inspect	Discuss	Solid
Gaze	Shout	Tremble
Glow	Amplify	Rough
Visible	Talk	Warm
Imagine	Whine	Shiver
Foresee	Call	Glow
Outlook	Articulate	Shake
Watch	Silence	Hold
See	Cry	Relax
Envision	Resounding	Move
Appear	Ring	Absorb
Glance	Mention	Flow
Notice	Said	Rush
Look	All reported speech	
All words describing colour		

There's a lot here, so take it easy and enjoy the discovery.

> **Bite 7**: Decide each day what you're going to look out for (Visual), listen for (Auditory), or get the feel of (Kinaesthetic), and keep to that. Once you start down this track, you'll find how much easier it is to notice ▶

> these aspects in other people and that means that you will be building not only your rapport skills but also your confidence; your confidence to speak to everyone.

> **Bite 8**: Start to match the other person's language patterns.

Matching in language (2)

Now you're getting the hang of matching language patterns, the last piece to tackle is matching key words and phrases.

We covered some of this in Chapter 3 as a strategy for keeping a conversation going, but it's well worth revisiting to make sure you realise the importance of it in relation to rapport.

Have you ever been in a situation where you have used a particular word or phrase to describe something and the person you're with has 'translated' it into their own words and you've got irritated, or at least found yourself wanting to say, 'That's not what I said', or 'That's not what I mean'?

> **You**: 'I just love barbeques.'
> **Them**: 'Yes al fresco dining can be such fun.'

> **You**: 'I could do with a break; work's been frantic.'
> **Them**: 'I know what it's like. We've been quite busy too.'

Inside you're just shouting, 'No!'

The lesson for us all? When someone uses a particular word or phrase to describe something, then the best way of building rapport is to use the same word or phrase in response.

> **Them**: 'I really hope they **work out** their problems.'
> **You**: 'I hope they **work them out** too.'

Or use them as a springboard for a question:

> **Them**: 'John's really **worried about** his exams.'
> **You**: 'What's he **worried about** particularly?'

If you can then couple your ability to identify and match their language patterns with your ability to pick up on some of the key words and phrases the other person uses you will have some tremendous tools for building rapport through language.

Now we're going to look at another element of rapport building called Pacing.

Pacing

Remember the two people in rapport walking down the street together? They are walking in step and when one speeds up, so does the other. They are, quite literally, pacing along with each other.

So the art of **pacing** is to do with following the person you are with wherever they go. And we don't mean jumping into a swimming pool fully clothed if that's what they do. Although that would be pretty strong evidence of rapport!

It's more to do with what we call pacing their current experience; pacing their emotional state; their feelings. Stepping into their world for a while so that you can get a better understanding of them and what they are experiencing.

You probably already know what it's like to have someone do this with you. You're feeling low and a friend let's you know that they understand how you feel and gives you the chance to express it. How do you feel towards them?

Something really great happens to you. You get the job you really wanted. You meet someone very special and all seems right with the world. You meet up with a friend who can see that something has happened, asks you about it, lets you ramble on and on about it and enters into the spirit of your experience with you. How do you feel towards them?

That is the power of pacing.

We're going to examine pacing in more detail when we give you some terrific strategies for talking in difficult situations in

Chapter 6, because you don't have to like someone to build rapport with them. Make a note of that:

"You don't have to like someone to build rapport with them."

In the meantime focus on the person you want to build rapport with for evidence, through their physiology and behaviour, of the state they are in and see how easy it is for you to pace them.

The next stage – pacing and leading

Once you have built a good level of rapport, you have the opportunity to lead. What is leading and when is it useful?

Leading is, very simply, using your rapport skills to shift the behaviour and state of the other person by modifying your behaviour. Remember the example of two people walking down the road in step? Well, if one of them speeds up, you'll find that the other speeds up as well, in order to keep up with their colleague. That is an example of pacing and leading.

Another example would be when you're speaking to someone who is maybe a bit 'down' and speaking very quietly and slowly. You match them for a while (pacing) then gradually start to speak a little more loudly and quickly. If they react to this and speed up as well as raising their volume, you have successfully 'led' them out of their state. This process is outlined in Figure 4.1. We are going to come back to this in Chapter 6 when we look at dealing with difficult situations.

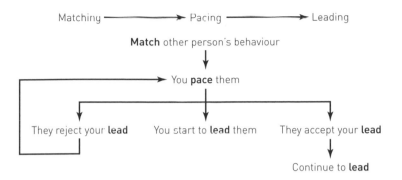

Figure 4.1 Match → pace → lead

Tips

1. *Notice what happens when people get on well. Look and listen for evidence of rapport in the way they tend to match.*
2. *Notice the opposite, when people are in disagreement. Look and listen for the evidence of their mis-matching.*
3. *Make it easy for others to communicate with you; practise rapport all the time.*
4. *Make it easy for yourself by practising one aspect at a time until your confidence grows in all areas.*
5. *Notice how you feel when you are matching different people.*
6. *Experience the world as the other person does – make them and their experiences/difficulties/joys much more understandable through pacing.*
7. *Remember that we get all sorts of information in body language and voice that is not there in the words.*
8. *Remember, too, that all this works fantastically well when you have integrity. People who 'do' rapport because they think it will help them get what they want but do it mechanically and with only self-interest in mind, are always found out.*

"You can't get away with false!"

Chapter

5

How you can talk to anyone at work

We meet a lot of people who love their work and an almost equal number of people who don't. And for those people who don't, the reason often lies not with the work itself but with their relationship, or lack of it, with colleagues and/or their boss. And even for those who do enjoy their work, there are often issues relating to other people that stop them enjoying it more.

Now, given that we spend two-thirds of our waking life at work, it makes sense that we should have the best time we can while we're there.

So this chapter is devoted to helping you to make the most of your working relationships, whether on a one-to-one or team basis, through offering you some terrific, proven, strategies that will allow you to talk to anyone at work with confidence.

Let's start with:

How to talk to your boss

Many people have problems talking to their boss. At least they have problems talking to them about things that really concern them. Reasons for this vary widely.

On what you might call a positive note, some people choose not to raise issues with their boss because they don't want to worry them; they think they've got enough on their plate already; they don't want to interrupt them or they're not sure of the best time to approach them.

On a less positive note, some don't do it because they think that nothing will happen if they do – apathy rules! – and there are then some more who think their boss won't do anything because they (the boss) are protecting their back and don't want to make waves.

Some think their boss will see it as sign of weakness/rebellion/whingeing, whilst others think they will see it as an attempt to curry favour (brown nosing again); some are simply scared to raise the issue because of the repercussions they think it may have on their future prospects and the way they will be treated.

Others just want to know how to get their point across in such a way that they are taken seriously and that something positive happens as a result.

Whatever group you fall into, here are some proven strategies for getting your point across and so build your confidence. Here's our blueprint for 'Talking to your boss'.

The first question to answer is, 'How does your boss like to be talked to?'

Stephen Covey, in his book *The 7 Habits Of Highly Effective People,* talks about the need '**to understand before being understood**'. In fact it's one of the seven habits that he identifies all truly successful communicators have. It's an indispensable first step in establishing any successful working relationship.

In which case, if you want to be able to talk to your boss effectively, you need to understand their style of communication and adapt accordingly.

Understanding your boss

It may be a blinding glimpse of the obvious but different people like to be talked to in different ways. They have different communication styles and preferred methods of communication. So what we're going to do is give you the chance to do some analysis of your boss's style and then give you the strategies you need to make the most of that information.

Here's our first 'Boss' exercise for you. We're going to give you a range of behaviours and your job is to decide where in that range your boss lies.

Exercise

You and your boss

Your boss's communication style:

Do they focus on:

The job _____ The people

Facts _____ Feelings

Detail _____Big picture

Are they:

Formal _____ Informal

Do they:

Use few gestures _____ Use lots

Use few facial expressions _____Use lots

Interrupt _____Let others talk

Tell _____Ask questions

Make quick decisions _____Take time to decide

Is their voice:

Monotone _____ Expressive

Now, once you've done this, you can start to work out how best to approach them and get the result that you want.

If your boss is more to the left of the range in the above exercise:

- focus on the job and getting the results that they are after
- be more formal in your approach
- talk to them about the job/results; show how you are helping them to achieve them

- when you're with them keep to the point and don't waffle
- if you have some ideas, present them in 'bullet point' form (not many of them) and leave them to make the decision as to which one they want
- give them facts and make sure your facts are right.

If your boss is more to the right of the range above:

- link anything you propose to the impact that it will have on the people
- show willingness to be sociable
- show them the 'bigger picture' impact
- look to build a relationship
- be less formal in your approach
- give your opinions and enthuse about them.

And all the while, be on the look-out for opportunities to build rapport through the skills you have developed in **matching**, **pacing** and **leading** (if you want to remind yourself of these go back to Chapter 4):

- Match gestures, posture, pace and tonality of voice, pausing.
- Then think about how your boss best likes to be communicated with. Do they prefer:
  - face-to-face (one-to-one, or one-to-group)
  - email
  - written
  - telephone?

And match your communication to their preferred method, still bearing in mind their style. So if they are to the left of the range, keep your emails short, bullet pointed and focus on the result. No chatty stuff about what you did at the weekend!

Keeping in touch

Once you've got a handle on your boss's communication style, your job is to build the best level of rapport that you can with them. And do remember this is a two-way street.

We meet people sometimes who go on and on about how difficult they find it to talk to their boss. One of the key messages they need to understand is that every relationship consists of two people and therefore both those people are contributing to it. If there are issues and difficulties, it is very rare that these are all attributable to only one person.

Most, if not all, issues/problems at work spring from communication breakdowns of some sort. And we would include lack of communication as a breakdown.

So the next thing to do, once you've developed some level of rapport – remembering that you don't necessarily have to like someone to have rapport with them – is to set up a system that keeps you in touch and keeps the communication channels open. And the best way to do this is to set up regular meetings with your boss.

For those of you who already have regular 1:1s with your boss, you'll appreciate the value of them. For those of you who don't and who have never had any, this can seem a bit of a challenge. The question in your mind is likely to be, 'How do I put it to my boss that I want to have regular meetings with them and get them to agree?' (Assuming, of course that you think it's a good idea! If you don't, please don't do it but don't then complain if things don't get any better.)

Later in this chapter we're going to give you **The 5 Point Blueprint For Getting Your Point Across** (page 108) as well as **The 1 MAT** (page 113) for putting together messages that people listen to. We suggest you use these to structure your message. But before you look at those, let's do some very important groundwork.

Getting your boss to say 'yes'

All too often people just run into a conversation and blurt out the thing that they want without thinking it through beforehand. And it's easy to understand why that might happen:

- they just want to get it off their chest
- they've been letting it 'stew' and the lid of the cooker blows

- they simply don't know how to plan it
- they tend to 'do things off the cuff'
- they don't see the value of planning communication.

At other times, of course, they decide it's just not worth the angst and the hassle and don't do anything about it. The problem then is that they only have themselves to blame if they're not happy with the situation. Do make sure that you really want to take action before embarking on this.

Hopefully you've got the message by now that the most successful and effective communicators DO plan things to the extent that they always know what they want to achieve from any communication or conversation. So this checklist will prove to be a useful reminder as well as giving you an easy to implement structure for planning to get what you want.

1. Work out what you want. Be absolutely clear about this. State it in the positive.

    'I want a regular (1 per week/per month, etc.) meeting with my boss.'

2. Work out what will be the evidence that you have achieved your outcome.

    'We will have agreed to meet on the last Tuesday of every month starting on 12 April.'

3. What will be the purpose of the regular meetings? Think through all the really good and valid reasons for having them.

4. What will be the positive consequences for you and your boss from having these regular meetings? You'll need to think this through bearing in mind what you know of your boss's style:

    - Do you need to emphasise the impact on results or on the people?

    - Do you need to provide some researched facts about the benefits of regular staff–boss meetings on productivity, etc?

    - Do you need to give some evidence of the positive opinions of other people who already have 1:1s with their boss?

5. What would be some of the potentially negative consequences of these meetings not taking place?

6. What's the best way of providing your evidence/making your points?

   - Do you need to produce a briefing document outlining your requirements/do a presentation?

   - Will it be more effective to talk it through informally?

7. Plan how best to make your request for the initial meeting:

   - When is your boss most likely to be available?

   - What is the best way of getting time in their diary?

   - Do you just pop your head round the door and ask?

   - Do you need to book a time via email?

   - Do you book a slot with their PA?

   - Do you need to send them anything in advance?

   - How important is it for them to have an agenda with timings attached?

8. Take some time to rehearse the meeting. We're going to give you another great strategy in Chapter 6 called '**The Three Chairs**' (if you want to have a look at it now you can find it on page 161) and you can use it here. It is a very powerful way of preparing for any communication by helping you to see things from different points of view.

Tip: Make no assumptions about your boss's reaction to this idea. Remember that we tend to get what we focus on and that if you think their response is likely to be negative that will be bound to influence the way in which you approach them.

Understanding your team

If you're a manager reading this, then we're going to guess that you will want to get the best out of each member of your team. Now, it may well be that you find it pretty easy to talk to them and if so, that's great. If you don't, then you'll want to find a way of doing that.

We're going to address that last issue now and then go on to give you a really tremendous and very simple strategy for talking to your team members and finding out what really motivates each one of them. That means that you will be able to get the absolute best from each of them and that can only be good for them, for you and for your business.

How to talk to your team

This is really a case of 'do as you would be done by'. If you think it's going to be useful for you to have 1:1 meetings with your boss, then guess what we're going to propose that you do? Exactly! Have regular 1:1s with each member of your team. And if you want to set these up and get buy-in from the team, then simply follow the process we've laid out above for you and your boss.

So let's assume that you've set up your conversations and you now want to find out how to get the best out of the team. Well, we've already given you the first step you need to take in Chapter 3. It's back to the question that begins, 'What's important ...?'

In this instance you want to find out what is important to them at work or in their job. Take some time to do this and you will reap the reward because you will then know what motivates them and what you need to do as their boss to keep their levels of motivation high. It will also give you the clues to look for if you see levels of motivation dropping.

Exercise

Finding the keys to your motivation

Find yourself a quiet spot where you will not be interrupted, get a pad and pen and write down your answers to the question:

'What's important to you in a job?'

Tip: Doing this with a colleague or friend can be even more beneficial as you can ask them to jot down your responses which leaves you to think it through without any distractions.

When you do this with someone else, just remember the ONLY questions you ask are:

'What's important to you in a job?'

'What else?' – to keep them going

'Is there anything else?' – when they tell you they've finished, just in case there is something they've left out.

Tip:
- *Don't comment or make judgements about anything on their list.*
- *Keep quiet and let them think.*
- *Write down ONLY the words that they use and use ONLY these words.*
- *Do not translate their words into your version, e.g. 'So being valued is important to you. Yes, it's the same for me, I like to be paid well for what I do.' That is NOT what they said!*

When we've asked this of people we work with we've had responses like:

- recognition
- job satisfaction
- being challenged
- the people
- helping customers
- being valued
- variety
- money
- having fun

- having a good boss
- … and many more.

Now, when you've got your list, here's the next question for you:

'Which of these values is the most important? If you could choose just one, which would it be?'

Once you've decided on that then do the same thing with all the rest until you have them all in order of priority. What you have then is a prioritised list of your values at work – the things that motivate you.

And the last thing you do is to take the list and ask one final question in relation to each item:

'What do I/you mean by.....?' or 'How would I/you know that I/you had ......?'

This question gives you the criteria by which you/they judge whether or not that value is being satisfied.

The thing that's important here is to recognise that we will all have different criteria attached to something to which we may give the same name. For instance, if 'recognition' is high on your list, how do you like to be recognised?

John and Laura both listed 'recognition' as a shared value. When we asked John, a member of the sales team, how he liked to be recognised, he said, 'Oh, at a team meeting. I want to be hauled up front with trumpets blaring!' At which point Laura practically sank from view under the table, her face covered with her hands.

'And how do you like to be recognised, Laura?' we asked her.

'Just a note in an envelope on my desk, please.'

Why is doing this and knowing this so important? Because most, if not all, of the big issues affecting someone's motivation at work are influenced by whether or not their values are being met. So, if you have a member of staff who is underperforming and has been doing so for any length of time, we're willing to bet the answer lies somewhere here. And if you have ever felt a deep level of dissatisfaction with work yourself, we're willing to bet the same.

Of course, if this is true of work, then it doesn't take a brain surgeon to work out that it is also true in other contexts; home life, social life, etc.

The reason for getting you to do this exercise is to give you a very powerful strategy for having really useful conversations with your team members. The questions are easy to ask, the information you get is like gold dust, because it tells you everything you need to know about how best to handle the person concerned. It gives you their key motivators, the buttons that you can press to get them performing at their best, and it also tells you where to look if things are not going so well.

As a side-effect, if you are dissatisfied at work, it may give you a better understanding of the reason for that. And once you have the understanding you can start to work out what you might need to do to put things right.

Everyone is different and knowing this, finding out where the differences lie, and responding to these differences are the things that mark out the great communicators. And just knowing this will give you an edge and will allow you to have wonderfully productive conversations with anyone you choose.

Tip: You can make these 1:1 meetings with your boss/team members really valuable as long as you decide what you want to get out of them.

So here's a checklist for a good, productive 1:1 meeting with your boss/team member:

- Make sure you/your boss has allocated time for the meeting.
- Have a very clear idea of what you want to get out of the meeting.
- Write this down and share it with your boss/team member before the meeting.

- Find out what he or she wants to get out of it.
- Ensure that every meeting ends with an agreed action plan.

Jeremy's story

Jeremy had a boss who made a habit of answering the phone during their 1:1 meetings.

One day Jeremy walked in for their meeting with a large stack of files under his arm.

'What are those for?' asked his boss.

'I thought I'd work through these while you're on the phone', said Jeremy.

His boss never took another phone call during a 1:1!

Now we're going to move on to give you some great strategies for getting your point across and making your voice heard in meetings and when you have to present ideas to a group of colleagues.

How to talk so people will listen

The 5 Point Blueprint For Getting Your Point Across

Getting your point across; getting your issue aired; getting your voice heard. There are going to be times at work when those become really important to you. The question is, how do you organise your thoughts and ideas in such a way that you make maximum impact and get the response that you want?

Firstly, it depends whether there's an issue or problem that you want to bring to people's attention, or whether you want to propose a solution to an existing and known problem.

Here are two very powerful formats. Besides being enormously helpful in the structuring of your argument, they both contain a hidden benefit.

People hate whiners. People like others to be positive. These formats offer you, if delivered in the right way (and that's up to you), a real chance to appear as a positive problem solver and solution seeker.

The first is useful when you want to bring an issue or problem to people's attention in order to convince them that it is worthwhile addressing and that it needs to be sorted out.

1. **State the problem:**
   - Identify the fact that the presentation will address itself to a problem.
   - Review or highlight key background points about the subject (that you know the group is either fully or partially aware of).
   - Clearly define the problem.

2. **Negative consequences:**
   - Identify the negative consequences that occur as a result of the problem. At this stage, keep your observations at a general and objective level; the specifics are coming later.

3. **Personal experience:**
   - Give examples and instances of your own experience of the problem and its impact on you.

4. **Evidence:**
   - Produce the facts and information which support and clarify the situation. This is the point at which you give the very specific details that will reinforce your position.
   - Use third-party evidence, beyond your personal experience. Here you produce the evidence that you will need to have gathered from colleagues, customers, suppliers; whoever else has been affected by the problem.

5. **Summary:**
   - Restate the problem as a headline to ensure that your audience has clarity.
   - Outline what action you believe needs to be taken to address/eliminate the problem.

You can use the next format when you have an idea or a recommendation that will solve **an already identified problem** and you want the audience to take action on your solution:

1. **Summarise the problem:**
   - Let your audience know that you have an idea that will solve an identified problem.
   - Briefly outline the problem.
   - Explain why it is a problem.

2. **Introduce your solution:**
   - Introduce your idea and explain how it relates to the problem.
   - Clarify your proposal.

3. **Positive consequences:**
   - Outline the positive consequences of implementing your solution. Ensure that these consequences are of value to your audience.

4. **Deliver the evidence:**
   - Produce the facts and information that provide the evidence of the value of your solution.

5. **Summary:**
   - Summarise the problem and the positive consequences of solving it.
   - Summarise your solution and the method of implementation.
   - Summarise the positive consequences of implementing YOUR solution.

6. **Action:**
   - Outline the action that needs to be taken, by whom and when.

Tip: Whichever situation you find yourself in, plan out your presentation carefully and, if possible, get a colleague/s to listen to it and give you feedback before you do it. This will go a long way to giving you added confidence. It will also give you a chance to test the validity and appeal of your solution and ensure that you are making your point clearly and unambiguously.

So now you have your message prepared, all you need to do is know:

How to get your audience's attention inside a minute!

Getting your entire audience's attention from the word 'go' is one of your main objectives. Yet how often do we hear introductions that do nothing to entice us and that sometimes actively turn us off? For example, 'Well I hope I don't bore you too much today....!' Well, there's a really powerful and very simple formula for engaging people straight away.

But before we give you the formula, we want to make you aware of your listening habits.

- How often have you been in a meeting at work and found your mind wandering?
- How often has someone started to contribute to a meeting and you have got lost in their introduction?
- How often have you – or someone else – been interrupted before you got to the real meat of what you were going to say?

If you were to examine any of these events you would probably find that the person speaking was using the following method to explain their idea or introduce their topic:

Introduction ———Main Topic/Attention Grabber ———Ideas

The problem here is that listening cycles work as shown in Figure 5.1:

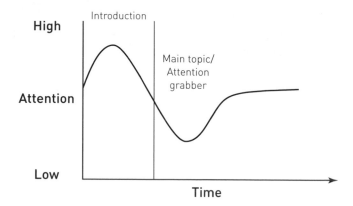

Figure 5.1 Attention span (1)

So, as you can see, in Figure 5.1 the main topic comes when then audience's attention is at its lowest ebb. If you want to make sure that your audience is really paying attention to you, then you need to start with your main topic or attention grabber and then give the details that support it, as shown in Figure 5.2.

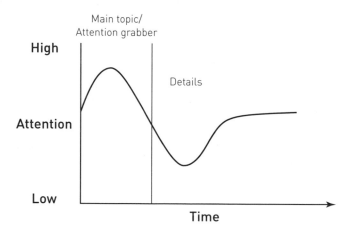

Figure 5.2 Attention span (2)

Now here's the formula for capitalising on this information:

The 4-MAT

The 4-MAT offers a very simple process and structure which is easy, powerful and effective. The structure is contained in four key questions and if you can answer all these questions within the first two to three minutes, you'll have your audience with you. The four questions are:

Why?

What?

How?

What if?

And here's the rationale behind the questions and the order in which you must answer them.

In any group you speak to you are going to find a mix of people for whom one of these questions is the most important. Just think for a moment ... which one do you want answered? Which one is the most important to you?

- Are you someone who has to know the reason for something before you will listen to the rest of the communication? Are you someone who wants to have an overview before you get into the detail? If so, you're a **Why?** person.

- Are you someone who wants information, who sees value in data to support ideas and proposals? If so, **What?** is your main focus.

- Are you someone who likes to know how things are going to work, likes solving problems, and enjoys hands-on involvement? **How?** does it for you.

- Are you someone who wants to know how to apply information in the future, likes action and trial and error and wants to be clear about the consequences of the action? The answers to the question **What if?** are crucial to you.

So, in relation to your presentation, think through and prepare your answers to these questions:

- Why are we here? Why are we addressing this issue? Why would the audience want to know about this?

- What are we going to be doing? What areas are we going to be covering? What will happen during the presentation?

- How are things going to pan out? How will I be able to use the information?

- What if I do? (What will I gain from this?) What if I don't? (What will be the consequences?) What if it happens? (What difference will it make?)

And **always remember** this:

"Answer the questions in the order we've given them to you!"

The key reason for this? If you don't answer **'Why?'** first, all of the 'Why?' people will simply turn off. They will not listen to you until you have given them a reason to do so. You don't necessarily need to spend ages doing it but you do need to address this question first.

4-MAT

Let's imagine that you've been asked to prepare a briefing/presentation about changes to some working practices:

Why?: 'As you all know, we've had feedback from customers and from you that some of our admin systems really need streamlining. We're falling behind with orders and to make sure we keep the customers we've got and attract new ones, we have to get smarter in the way we do certain things.'

What?: 'So we're going to examine all our current systems and ways of working, particularly those that involve us working together across departments.'

How?: 'In order to make sure we get everyone's voice heard, we're going to set up a working group in each department that will be responsible for getting all your thoughts and feeding

---

them back into the management team. This will happen over the next month and we'll have proposals ready by the second week in May.'

What if?: 'Now some of you are bound to have questions as we go along and rest assured that we will give you the opportunity to ask them. We have to ensure that whatever solutions we arrive at are workable and give you the best chance of delivering great customer service. The only way we can do that is to make it easier for you to do your jobs well.'

If you think you might meet any resistance, or want to get an even higher level of attention and buy-in, you can always start with a **'Yes' set** (see below).

Do all this and you will have a great introduction already written that you know is going to hit all the 'hot buttons' in your audience. And just think how much more confidence that will give you!

Now sometimes you may find yourself wanting to put your ideas forward to a group who are not very receptive. And that can be quite daunting, especially if presenting to groups is not your forte. The temptation can be to try to ignore the less enthusiastic people, the cynics, and focus on the friendly faces. By doing that you miss out on a great opportunity to get your message across to everyone. So here's a strategy to help you win friends and give you confidence whoever you find yourself talking to.

'Yes' sets

'Yes' sets are a series of statements which everyone in the group you are talking to is going to find it easy to agree with. The purpose of a 'Yes' set is:

- to create an environment of agreement
- to get your group used to agreeing with you
- to show them that you understand their situation
- to build rapport.

Let's take a very general example. You might say to a group of business people:

'The situation in the economy at the moment is exceptionally challenging and all of you are finding yourself in a far more competitive environment. You are busy people and I know you want to make the best use of your time today.'

There are a number of statements there which will resonate with your audience:

- 'Is the economy challenging?' **Yes.**
- 'Are they in a more competitive environment?' **Yes.**
- 'Are they busy people?' **Yes.**
- 'Do they want to make the best use of their time?' **Yes.**

So, by the time you have finished this very brief introduction, your audience will have said 'Yes' to you four times.

So, if you want to use the 'Yes' set, build a series of statements with which your audience can only agree. Take advantage of your knowledge of their current situation and use the 'Yes' set to reinforce your position.

If you do have people there who may not be receptive for whatever reason, you can still bring them into the 'Yes' set.

Example:'Yes' set

'I know you're all really busy and you've got a whole heap of work to do before the end of the week. [Yes × 2]

I know that some of you are keen to hear our ideas for a new way of streamlining the department's procedure [Yes from those who are] whilst others of you think that it would be better to carry on doing it the way we have been [Yes from those who aren't]. And I totally understand that.

Change is not always a good thing [Yes from everyone] but if it can deliver a better way of doing things [Yes from some] and get rid of some of the processes that have created problems for you in the past [Yes from others], then it might be well worth considering, don't you reckon?

And whether you're keen to change things or not, I appreciate you giving up the time to be here and can promise that before we do make any changes you will all have the opportunity to have your views heard.'

Whilst you may not have got people to change their minds, you will at least have engaged them and demonstrated that you understand their point of view.

Handling questions

One of the times that people come unstuck when they are talking to groups, or individuals, is when taking questions. And, of course, question time can come along when you least expect it.

Tip: Whenever you're going to do a presentation and you know there are going to be questions, particularly if you think that there may be some people who are less than enthusiastic about what you are going to propose, there is one strategy you MUST follow:

Brainstorm the questions you think you will be asked and PLAN your answers.

Doing this will give you so much more confidence.

If you're doing a presentation to a work group, or a client, your best course of action is to make sure that you let them know right at the start of your presentation what you intend to do about questions. Basically you have three options:

1. You take all questions at the end. So you would say something like:

   'I know you'll have questions and I'm going to allow time at the end of my presentation/talk for that. So I'd be grateful if you would just jot down any questions that arise and I'll be happy to address them then.'

2. You take questions as you go. The advantage of this is that people can raise their issues, have them dealt with, and then they have cleared their minds as you move on. The down side is that you have far less control over time and you might find yourself having to stop questions so that you can finish on time. It's your decision.

3. For anyone who may do business presentations to clients, we have evolved a very effective strategy for questions. We say to the group at the start: 'We know that you will have questions at the end of our presentation and we're going to propose that we take a break then to give you time to talk through the issues you want to raise with us. How useful would that be for you?' Not everyone has taken us up on this offer but it has proved to be particularly effective with those who have.

Whichever route you take, you will arrive at question time and here are our top tips for handling questions:

- If you get a multiple part question, split it up and answer one part at a time. You can also ask your questioner, 'Which part of your question would you like me to answer first?' This will tell you which part the questioner regards as the most important. Answer this effectively and quite often the other parts will become irrelevant.

- Pay particular attention to the body language and tone of voice of the person asking the question. This will give you a very good indication of their intentions.

- Make sure you understand the question before you answer it. If there is anything you are unclear about, ask for clarification.

- With larger groups, it is worth repeating the question to ensure that everyone understands it. If necessary, perhaps with a complex question, rephrase it to make it simpler. You can use a phrase such as, 'Let me just make sure I understand your question. Are you asking … ?'

- Eye contact should be around 40 per cent for the questioner and 60 per cent for the rest of your audience.

- Use the questioner's name when responding.

- **If you can't answer, don't!** No flannelling allowed! Simply admit that you don't know the answer and commit to getting one within an acceptable timescale. Make sure you do!

- Check with your questioner that they are happy with your answer: 'Does that answer your question?' 'Are you happy with that?'

- If you need time to think, **pause!** Take your time. Take a sip of water. Keep your body language positive and relaxed. It's even more evidence of confidence.

- If you are allowing questions during the presentation and someone asks about an issue that you know will be covered later, then tell them that you will be providing the answer at that time. Move on.

- Turn negative questions into simple requests for information. If someone asks, 'Why on earth is it going to take you so long to do the research?', instead of repeating the question and reinforcing the negative aspects, say something like; 'You want to know more about how we intend to go about the research phase. Here's our rationale ...'

- Avoid repeating any negative or hostile words.

- If someone in your audience leaps to a conclusion that is false or makes an assumption that you had not intended them to make, you must correct them.

- Likewise, if someone tries to take you off track with a question, politely bring them back into line.

- If you get a question veiled as an attack, try to find what's behind it – more on handling difficult situations in Chapter 6. 'Thank you for the question. I'm interested to know your reason for asking it.'

- When you come to the end, thank everyone for the opportunity to answer their questions and clarify their thinking.

- We always add one more question. 'Before we finish, is there anything else?' More often than not, the answer is, 'No.' But sometimes we have uncovered a gem, and it has paid dividends. We leave it with you as an option.

- **Whatever else you do:**
  - Keep It Simple.
  - Keep It Focused.
  - Keep In Control.

External networking

The very word 'networking' can strike fear into the souls of some. We know people who will do whatever they can to avoid attending what they see as these life-threatening events!

So much of our experience is based on how we view things. Think again of the different effect the words 'presentation' and 'conversation' has had on some of the people we have worked with. Let's apply the same principle to 'networking'.

What is networking and what is its purpose? Well, as we see it networking is what we're doing pretty much all the time. The only differences are the contexts in which we do it.

- Is a party networking?
- Is being on a training course a networking opportunity?
- Is attending a conference networking?
- Is a reunion of old school friends networking?

The answer to all of these is, 'Yes'. Well, it's 'Yes' if you accept our premise that networking is all about building and fostering successful relationships.

Now quite clearly we are going to feel more comfortable in some of the contexts above that we are in others. The secret is to be able to transfer the level of comfort we feel with our friends at a party to other gatherings where we are less familiar with the people there.

We've already covered in Chapter 3, 'Conversation basics' a number of really effective strategies that will serve you well in any context and networking is one of those.

All the best networkers that we know are good listeners and questioners. They are innately curious and like to learn about other people. They also go to every networking event they attend with very clear objectives. So remember that what we've done already still counts!

If you want to become even more confident, see networking events – whatever the context – as a real opportunity to expand your business or social contacts, and look forward to them with a sense of anticipation, then here are some golden nuggets for you. Implement these and you'll never look back!

Starting points

Predominantly, of course, networking is seen as a way of forming business contacts through informal social gatherings. Now this may be what you want to do but, if you're introverted by nature, you don't have to start by summoning up your courage and throwing yourself in at the deep end. That way leads to stress, anxiety and ultimately a dislike of anything to do with networking.

It may be that you want to begin networking for your own ends or it may be that it is part of your job and that you are expected to network on behalf of your company.

Whichever of these descriptions best fits you, let's consider the easiest ways to begin the journey to becoming confident in any networking situation.

1. **Start with people you know:** If your purpose is to expand the number of business contacts you have, then start with people you already know. These may be friends or people you have already met in a business environment.

   How about trying old school friends, attending gatherings of ex-students, rekindling old friendships? Of course, you don't even have to talk to them in these days of Facebook, LinkedIn and the other social networking sites. At least it's a start.

   Always remember that if someone is present at any sort of networking event, their objective is to meet new people, so you're all in the same boat!

2. **Go where you enjoy going:** Great places to begin networking are those where people of similar interests gather. Are you keen on any particular sport? Do you have a hobby or interest? Do you enjoy music? Do you love walking?

   Where do people who have similar interests to yours gather? Since we know that people like people like them – see Chapter 4 on building rapport – you will find it much easier to engage in conversation around a shared interest or passion.

3. **Making the most of it:** OK, let's assume now that you are about to attend a business networking event and you want to make the most of it. There are three stages to consider:

   - preparation
   - participation
   - follow-up.

Let's take them one by one.

Preparation

Think about why you're going. What do you want to get out of the event? What's your purpose? What can you take from the event that will be of real value to you and your business?

Prepare your introduction. One of the things you can be absolutely certain of is that you will be asked who you are and what you do. This gives you an opportunity to make a positive impact – take it! And here are some tips for a great introduction:

1. Make it brief. People don't have time and don't want to listen to the history of your company since its formation in 1923. You've got 15 seconds at most! Write it out, time it and rehearse it until it feels entirely comfortable.

2. Don't tell them what your company **does**, tell them what it **achieves** and by doing this you also spell out the benefits of doing business with you. For example:

   'I'm John Smith. I work for ABC Accountancy. We help small businesses maximise their profitability and minimise their tax burden.'

'I'm Jill Brown. I'm with XYZ Software. We design IT solutions that deliver 100 per cent accurate customer activity information for retail businesses.'

'I'm Tim Fearon. I'm co-owner of The Extraordinary Coaching Company. We help small to medium sized companies find the hidden money in their business.'

If you're going to an event on your own behalf, to network for a new job, then prepare your **personal** introduction. Again, it needs to be brief and it needs to sell the benefits that you will bring to the business. It is NOT an opportunity to talk them through your CV and the last 15 years of your employment history. Again, write it out, time it and rehearse it. You also need to plan your answers to any question you may be asked, such as, 'Why are you looking to move jobs?'

Check with others in your business who will not be attending what contacts they would like you to make on their behalf. This is a great strategy, because it allows you to use them as a valid reason for approaching the named contact.

Take some time to look through the agenda for the event, if there is one, and the various sessions on offer. Choose those that you reckon will be most beneficial and then set outcomes for each of those sessions. What specifically do you want to learn/understand/be able to do/do as a result of attending that session?

At the same time that you are looking through the agenda, study the delegate list if the event organiser hasn't provided one, call them and ask them if they can provide you with one.

Decide who you want to make contact with and the reason for making contact with them. Research their company so you have some salient details handy for your conversation. Do this well and it provides you with your 'ice-breaker' when you first make contact. You can then plan your 'ice-breaker' – an opening remark or question. The questioning areas you may want to plan for could include:

- their business background
- how long they have been in the business

- how and why they started
- what have been their best/most difficult moments
- how many years have they been in the industry
- the state of their business in the current environment
- the main challenges facing them
- their main competitors
- their future plans and ambitions.

Give yourself a realistic target for the number of people you want to meet. Then decide when and how you will make contact with them. Of course you may want to meet up with the 'usual suspects', that's part of the joy of these events, but there will be other opportunities for meeting people who could be of enormous value to your business in the future.

And thinking about the 'usual suspects', avoid the temptation to spend all your time with them because it makes life easy.

Decide on how you will judge whether or not the event has been a success. How will you know it has been worthwhile? What do you want to walk out of the doors with at the end that you didn't have at the beginning and how will you know that you have it?

On a practical front, make sure that you are well equipped with business cards, something to write on and pens. Why more than one pen? You can bet your bottom dollar that you'll meet someone who has forgotten theirs. Enjoy the moment when you offer them one of yours. You'll never have a problem getting them to answer the phone the next time you want to talk to them!

It's worth preparing yourself for those moments when people reject your approaches; those people who can't or who don't want to listen to you. As they say on the T-shirt 'Stuff Happens'. It's not personal, it's business. Move on and leave it behind.

Finally, have fun! OK, we realise that may sound like we're asking a lot, but if you implement everything we've given you, you really will start to enjoy yourself; and that's a promise!

Besides ensuring that you get value from the event, completing this 'checklist' has another really positive result. It means that you will be focused on achieving your goals and getting hold of all the information and people that you have targeted. This means that your focus of attention will be on other people and not on yourself. You won't have time to be nervous or anxious!

Participation

If you're not used to networking events, or find them daunting, the first rule is:

"Make it easy for yourself."

1. If for any reason, you feel tense or anxious before you enter the room, here are some great tips:
   - Take a moment in private and stand in the 'right position' that we established in Chapter 3: stand up straight; keep your head erect.
   - Adopt and maintain an assertive stance: stand with your feet hip width apart; keep your weight evenly balanced.
   - When walking, walk with purpose.
   - Breathe deeply and easily. Breathing deeply – from your diaphragm as opposed to your upper chest – sends a signal to the brain that you are relaxed and confident.
   - Establish a rhythm of breathing whereby you are taking twice as long to breathe out as you are to breathe in, e.g. breathe in to a count of five and out to a count of ten.
   - Notice how much more relaxed you feel after half a dozen or so breaths.
   - Hold this feeling and walk into the room.
2. Introduce yourself to people who are on their own. This will allow you to warm up and get familiar with the environment and practise your skills in a relaxed fashion.
3. Approach smaller groups. This makes it easier for you to introduce yourself and engage with the individual members.

4. Remember again that what we've done already still counts! Here's your chance to employ your skills of listening, questioning and curiosity that we developed together in Chapter 4.

5. Find out as much as you can about the people you are with and be prepared to offer any information, contacts, etc. That may be useful to them.

6. Ask for their business cards so that you can:

   ● remember their names

   ● have a record of who you talked to and how to reach them

   ● use the back of the card to write down what you talked about, so that when you follow up you can remind them of your conversation.

7. Always read their business card to make sure all the relevant information for contacting them is there.

8. If you think you are going to want to contact them again in the future, ask their permission to do so.

9. Top tips for 'difficult situations':

   ● If your conversation reaches its natural end, or simply dies out, excuse yourself and move on. You can always say something along the lines of, 'It's been great to meet you. There are a number of other people I need to make contact with, so I hope you'll excuse me.'

   ● If you run into someone you've already met and can't remember their name, simply say 'Hello again. Remind me of your name' and then remind them of yours.

   ● If you find yourself back with someone you that you don't want to spend any more time with, ask if they've met anyone especially interesting that you might like to meet. Or point out someone who you found interesting that might be useful for them to meet.

Follow-up

Follow up within 24 hours of the event. Most follow-up seems to be done via email or phone call these days. If you want to make an impact, follow up with a handwritten note. Whatever else happens, they'll remember you.

If you follow this system, it makes the next point of contact so much easier and you can lift the phone with the confidence that they are far more likely to want to speak with you.

6 Chapter

How to talk to anyone in difficult situations

Even for the confident communicator, there will be certain 'difficult situations' that put their skills to the test. We all have examples of conversations or people that we find more challenging. And these people can be family members, clients, customers or work colleagues.

Whether it's dealing with aggressive behaviour, standing up for ourselves, trying to talk to someone when emotions are running high or simply asking for what we want, there are going to be times when we feel out of our comfort zone and exposed.

In this chapter we're going to cover some of the general principles that apply to pretty much any difficult situation and give you strategies that you can employ 'anywhere, anytime' and then we're going to look at some very specific situations and the strategies and tools that you can employ to bring you success.

Let's start with the general principles and first is one of the fundamental beliefs of effective communicators:

"All behaviour has a positive intention."

What this means is that everything we do, however strange it may seem to someone else, we do for a reason which is positive for us, otherwise we wouldn't do it.

Have you ever had moments when someone has done something, behaved in a certain way, and you've thought to yourself, 'Why on earth did they do that?', or 'What do they hope to achieve by behaving like that?' If you have, join the rest of us.

However behind that behaviour is – believe it or not – a positive intention. They are getting something out of behaving that way or, and this is **very important**, they are hoping to get something out of behaving that way. What is that intention? Well, until you know, you can only guess.

Why is it valuable to know this? In situations where we are faced with 'difficult' or challenging behaviour, it can be very easy to react and respond to the behaviour. Sometimes, this means springing to our own defence. Sometimes it can result in confrontation. Sometimes it can end in tears.

If you want to be the best you can be in these situations, then here's the secret:

"Find the positive intention!"

Don't react to the behaviour but go on the search – 'truffle hunting,' as one great communicator we worked with termed it – for the intention that lies behind the behaviour. How to do that? Let us give you a quick example – here is Bill's story.

Bill's story

John was setting up to run a sales development workshop in a client's offices one day and one of the staff, called Joyce, was helping him. He had his back to the door when he heard it opening and Joyce said, 'John, this is Bill. He's on the workshop today.' Now John's a pretty friendly guy, so he turned round, put out his hand to shake Bill's, and said, 'Good morning, Bill.'

Well, we can't write out here what Bill said because this book would never get past the censor! But he just let rip about the waste of his ******* time, how sales training didn't ******* work, how it was flavour of the ******* month, how much ******* work he had to do and every other word was ******* unprintable!

Now one thing you know as well as we do; storms blow themselves out. So John just stood there and waited. Although every bone in his body wanted to react and he just wanted to say,

'Well, Bill, if you feel like that, maybe it would be better for you to get on with your work instead of being here.'

Anyway, the storm did blow itself out. When he had finished, John just looked at him – he had nothing to lose – and said, '*So, Bill, I wonder what lies behind all of that*?' It was as if he had hit him. Bill swayed backwards and after a pause said, 'I get claustrophobia. I can't stand being in small rooms like this with a lot of people.' **Wow!** One great reason – **positive intention** – for not wanting to be there.

They got talking and John found out that on the last sales training he'd attended the trainer had made him look like an idiot in front of his colleagues! **Wow again!** Another great reason – **positive intention** – for not wanting to be there.

So what happened?

John made sure Bill got a seat near the door, plenty of water available, and told him that if he felt he needed to leave at any time then he should do just that and he would understand. He also explained that he operated in a very different way from the previous trainer.

Bill stayed for the entire two days, never had to leave the room, and was a great contributor to the workshop! And on the last day, when everyone had left and John was clearing up, the door opened and there was Bill. 'You know, John, that wasn't half ******* bad!' Now, that was a result!

What would have happened if John had responded to his behaviour and suggested that Bill get on with his work and miss the workshop? Bill would have got the result he wanted. His positive intentions would have been fulfilled.

We're not going to suggest it's always as easy as this, but it's always worth trying. It's always worth trying to find the positive intention that is driving the behaviour.

And the best way to do it is to ask a question. In Bill's story the question John asked was, 'What lies behind all of that?' That doesn't mean it was the best or the only question he could have asked. The reason it was a good question was because it worked; it got the result John was after. Remember what Krishnamurti said:

"The information that you want is in the question you intend to ask."

So what other questions could you ask to find the intention behind the behaviour?

Here are some ideas:

'What's your purpose in doing that/behaving like that?'

'What are you hoping to achieve by doing that/behaving in that way?'

'What's in it for you when you do that?'

'When you behave like that, what do you get from it?'

Some of these questions might sound a bit strange to you. You might find yourself thinking, 'but that's not the way I talk'. And that's absolutely fine to think that way. It probably isn't the way you have talked in the past. But then maybe you've never asked that kind of question hoping to get the kind of information it generates.

And here's something you need to know. Very few people, in our experience, ask these kind of questions and very, very, few people have ever been asked them. The result is that, more often than not, when you ask these questions, you get the answer you're looking for.

One other thing you might notice in Bill's story, is that when John asked the question, 'What lies behind all of that?' he prefaced it with, 'So Bill, I wonder …' This is another great strategy that 'takes the edge off' the question. It softens it somehow and makes it less confrontational than it could be and demonstrates John's curiosity rather than his bewilderment! And curiosity is one of the qualities that you want to develop.

Now for another fundamental belief of truly effective communicators:

"The meaning of my communication is the response that I get."

The purpose of this belief is to acknowledge that we are responsible, entirely responsible, for the reactions that our communication generates. This means that we have a part to play in every relationship and interaction that we have.

Sometimes, particularly in difficult situations, we can blame the other person for the problem. You'll have heard people say things like:

'They're just impossible to talk to.'

'Things would be fine if they would only change.'

'They're really difficult.'

'I give up, they're always the same.'

Now we know that some people are a heck of a lot more challenging than others. Are you one of those people, by the way?

But what we all have to accept is that whenever we are in communication with another person, we are part of what's going on. We are part of the system and if we want things to be different, here's the thing; something in the system has to change.

You'll have heard the saying:

'If you always do what you've always done, you'll always get what you always got.'

Or, put another way, as Albert Einstein put it when he defined insanity:

'It's doing the same thing time after time after time and expecting a different result.'

If you find yourself in a situation/relationship where you are consistently getting a result that you don't want, you need to realise that you are, in some way, contributing to that situation/relationship. And the great thing is, that once you acknowledge this, you can start to do something about it.

Which leads us rather neatly to the third fundamental belief of truly effective communicators:

"The person with the most flexibility in any relationship will be the catalyst for change."

Simply put, whoever is most easily able to change the way they are doing things is going to be the one who creates change, because the reason so many people get stuck in relationships that are counterproductive is that neither – assuming we are talking about a two-person relationship for the moment – is sufficiently flexible to stop what they're doing/the way they're behaving, and do something different.

We come across this a lot; at work, in social situations, in partnerships and marriages. And, interestingly enough, the reason we are often given for a person not changing is, 'If I stop/change, it'll look like I've given in'. And so the reason for not changing has a positive intention behind it: the desire not to appear weak.

But if you think about it, the converse is true. The person who recognises that something has to shift; the person who takes the initiative; the person who creates a new and better way of doing things is not weak. They are the strength that the other person needs to assist them to move on. And, to be frank, they are the one who has the more positive of intentions.

And so they make a change and nothing happens, or at least not the thing they were hoping for. Now what? Enter the fourth fundamental belief of truly effective communicators:

"All outcomes are achievements of some kind; there is no failure, only feedback."

And this one can be a challenge for us all. If we're honest, we've probably got the T-shirt already.

It's a tough call to do something you've really geared yourself up to do; gathered all the resources you could; gone and done it and it hasn't worked, to then turn round and say to yourself: 'OK, so that didn't work. It's just information and what am I going to do with it? What could I have done differently that could have made a difference? What can I learn? What does that mean for the next time that I try to make that change?' Because sometimes all you want to do is sit down and cry or bash your head against the nearest brick wall, wailing, 'I tried so hard and I've failed! Well, that's the last time I go out of my way for them!'

It's very tempting to walk away. But stay. The rewards are tremendous. And, there may be times that, even with all your efforts you are unable to create the outcome you want. But be sure of one thing. You will have learnt an enormous amount about yourself and will have expanded the options you have in the future and that means that you will have more choices in your life. And if this book achieves only that one thing and helps you to understand that you always have a choice and develops your ability to make great choices, it will have been more than worth it.

The final piece in the 'anywhere, anytime' category is to do with mindset:

"Thinking 'difficult' makes it 'difficult'."

We spent some time in Chapter 1 looking at what makes someone socially confident and this is a great opportunity to put that understanding into action.

Let's assume that we're going to be engaging in a difficult conversation of some sort. One of two things usually holds good. We either know it's coming, or it takes us by surprise. If we know it's coming, then we can prepare ourselves.

The three steps to success or 'prepare for the best'

1. Know what you want, not what you don't want

This is vital; that you are absolutely clear what you want from the conversation.

You'll remember that in Chapter 1 we stressed the importance of knowing what you want as opposed to knowing what you don't want. In a difficult situation it's very tempting to keep thinking about the things you don't like about it. You focus on the negative aspects of the relationship and wish them away.

The problem is that as long as you focus on the negative aspects, that's what you're going to keep getting, because that's what you're focusing on! So you have to shift your focus and that means that you need to take some time out before you have the conversation to think through what you really want to happen as a result of it. It's a good idea to go one step further here and write it down. And make sure that you phrase it in the positive. Just note the difference between the two outcomes below:

> 'I want him to understand how I feel about the issue and recognise that the way he is behaving is upsetting me. I want him to understand what I want him to do differently and what I will do on my part to change the way we communicate.'

As opposed to:

> 'I don't want him to ignore me anymore and I don't want him to keep upsetting me.'

In the first example the focus is all on the positive outcomes of the conversation and the future state of the relationship, whilst in the second example the focus is on the negative aspects of the relationship and is rooted in the problem.

2. Rehearse having it already

This is a major part of preparing for success, and you'll need to set aside some time for doing this, just as Mohammad Ali did when he created his 'future history'. We've got some really terrific strategies for you here and we are going to leave it up to you to experiment with them to find out which work best for you.

Write the play

Find somewhere quiet where you won't be disturbed and make yourself comfortable.

Start thinking about the conversation you are going to have and summon up as many details as you can:

- where it will take place – the room, layout of the room, etc.
- the day and time of day
- the person, or people, you will be having the conversation with
- what you will be doing immediately before the conversation
- how the two of you – if there are going to be more of you, then bring the others in as well – will be seated or arranged in the room.

In other words, get a picture in your mind of the forthcoming event and make it as rich in detail as you possibly can. Now enrich it even further by adding colours and sounds.

Once you have a really well-formed image – this is the internal representation that we talked about in Chapter 2 – start to rehearse the event, holding in your mind all the time the positive outcome that you have already formulated:

- put yourself in the picture, as if you were there
- add in all the detail you need to make it as realistic as you can
- run the conversation through just the way you want it to go

- notice, as you move towards your outcome, the positive feelings that you start to experience
- run it through all the way to a successful conclusion, with you leaving the room, your outcome achieved.

Once you have done this, run it again three or four times, or more if you want to, until, like Mohammad Ali, you get it 'into the muscle'.

It's behind you! (for those of you who like pantomimes!)

This strategy is particularly useful if there is a specific situation or individual that you find difficult and you want to change the way you feel about it or them.

Firstly, get a picture in your mind of the situation or person and then imagine you're in a theatre and the person is on the stage. And now, move your seat so that the stage is way below you – you're sitting in the gods – and the person is now really quite small. And as you watch them on the stage, all the way down there, they start to break into a silly dance and before you know what's happened they've become a character for one of your favourite comic books!

And as this happens, just notice what happens to your feelings about them.

Change the picture

Whenever we create an internal representation of anyone, as we discovered in Chapter 4, we create it in three ways:

- Visual.
- Auditory.
- Kinaesthetic.

Using this knowledge we can create a different internal representation by changing the quality of the picture. It's a bit like playing around with a television picture.

So, for example, we can change the images (**Visual**) by changing:

- location – where the picture is in relation to us; close or far away; to the left or to the right, etc.
- associated or dissociated – are you in the picture with them or are you looking at yourself in the picture?
- brightness
- colours – is it in colour or black and white; are the colours bright or dim?
- size of image
- movement.

We can change the sounds (**Auditory**) by changing:

- location
- volume
- tempo
- pitch
- rhythm, etc.

And we can change the feelings (**Kinaesthetic**) by changing:

- location – is the feeling in our stomach or in our chest?
- shape – does it have a size or a shape?
- size
- temperature
- movement – does the feeling move around or is it located in one place?

We've given you a checklist below of some of the characteristics of the pictures, sounds and feelings that you can change. Use this when you do the next exercise and see what you can discover.

Exercise

In your mind's eye

Think of someone that you find less than easy to deal with and as you do that, simply write in the columns below the characteristics of your internal representation of them.

When you do this you may discover that there is one characteristic which, when you change it, the others change automatically. Keep your eyes and ears open for it.

Visual

Location			
Associated or dissociated			
Bright or dim			
Framed or panoramic			
Colour or black and white			
Size of picture			
3D or flat			
Intensity of colour			
Degree of contrast			
Movement or still			
In focus or not			
Angle viewed from			
Number of pictures			

Auditory

Location			
Tonality			
Volume			
Tempo			
Pitch			
Rhythm			

Inflections (words marked out)			
Pauses			
Timbre (quality)			
Uniqueness of sound			
Direction			
Duration			
Internal or external			

Kinaesthetic

Location			
Shape			
Size			
Temperature			
Movement or still			
Texture			
Vibration			
Pressure			
Duration			
Steady or intermittent			
Intensity			
Weight			
Internal or external			

Exercise

Changing pictures

Now think of the person from the previous exercise again and start to make some changes to the picture.

So, for example, if the image was close to you, move it away. If it was in colour, turn it into black and white. If it was moving, make it still. If you were in the picture, participating, come outside as if you were looking in, watching yourself participating.

If there was sound, turn it down or off. If the sound was harsh, make it soft and soothing.

If the feeling was inside you see if you can move it outside you. If it was moving, make it still.

If, of course, you have found the one characteristic that, when you change it, everything else changes, use it first.

In any event, once you have made the changes just notice what happens to you. How do you feel now about this person?

Tip: We've noticed that when people are thinking about someone whom they view as intimidating, in a position of authority over them, then more often than not they will place the visual image somewhere above them.

If this is the case, they get a real shift in their feelings simply by moving the picture down and further away from them. They often achieve another big shift by turning the picture into a still one, if it has been moving and by turning it into black and white if it has been in colour.

Experiment for yourself and have some fun. Whatever else happens, they'll never look the same again!

3. Let's do consequences

If you need any added motivation to tackle the issue or have the conversation, then give yourself a few more minutes' reflection time. Just consider what the positive consequences will be for you achieving your outcome – write them down. And then think through the negative consequences of your not achieving your outcome. Write these down as well. Compare the lists.

Now ask yourself these three all important questions:

- Is it worth it?
- Do I want it?
- Do I really, really want it?

If the answer to these is 'Yes', you're on your way. You'll do it.

If the answer is, 'I'm not sure' then go back and repeat what you've just done, asking yourself how you'd know you were sure.

If the answer is 'No', then just accept the facts as they are and live with it. But don't ask for your money back!

The everyday toolkit

Now we've covered some of the basic principles, let's examine some specific examples of 'difficult situations'; situations which may come upon you suddenly, without warning, such as:

- handling angry/aggressive people
- handling passive, shy, unforthcoming people
- standing up for yourself
- getting away from the 'Bores of Britain'.

Handling Mr (or Ms) Angry

Here are two great strategies for this situation.

Go truffle hunting

It's a bit of a challenge at times like this, but one great strategy is to go searching for the positive intention. Remember, 'all behaviour has a positive intention'.

The questions that go behind the behaviour are often real 'stop them in their tracks' type questions. The fact is, they're unexpected and they form what we call in our trade, a pattern interrupt. This is a response that is completely left-field and that the other person just doesn't see coming.

The result is that it interrupts the flow of their thinking and behaviour and that means that they have to change tack in order to respond to it.

Be an adult

It's OK, we know you're an adult. Your challenge, particularly in difficult situations, is to stay an adult and stop being sucked into behaviour that is not going to get you the result that you want.

Let's just think for a minute about some of the situations that people find challenging:

- dealing with figures of authority
- standing up for themselves in the face of aggressive behaviour
- handling grown up tears and tantrums!
- dealing with 'experts' who think they know it all
- making a complaint.

There may well be others, but that's probably enough to be going on with. The thing is that, regardless of the specific situation, behaviours, reactions and responses tend to form a few general clusters that are pretty easy to recognise.

Before we start to look at these, a quick reminder that:

"All behaviour has a positive intention."

The importance of this in the context of 'challenging behaviour' is that the person who is exhibiting the behaviour is doing it because they want to get something out of it that is positive for them.

Now, we may not know EXACTLY what it is that Mr (or Ms) Angry are after. As this is not a book about the search for the underlying causes of behaviour that may or may not emanate from someone's childhood experiences, we are not interested in discovering the root cause of behaviour. What we are interested in is giving you more choice in the way in which you respond to people who display certain 'challenging' behaviours. So what we're going to do is to consider some of these, outline the options you have in the moment, and give you the strategies you need to handle them successfully.

What you may have noticed already is that we are talking about 'challenging' behaviours and not 'challenging' people. And we find this is a really useful distinction to make. After all, even you may from time to time display behaviours that are less than, how shall we put it, attractive! But you're not like that all the time, are you? And because you behave like that on some occasions, as Rod Steiger the American actor once famously said in the film *No Way To Treat A Lady*, 'It doesn't mean you're a bad person!'

How often have you heard people say things like:

'She didn't even say hello to me this morning, she's so rude.'

'I heard him shouting at the builders yesterday, he's a nightmare.'

'The doctor wouldn't give me an appointment today. She's so unhelpful.'

What these people have done is to take a behaviour and turn it into a statement about the other person's identity. In other words, they have given them a label. The problem with this is that they are now quite likely, in future conversations and meetings, to go into those conversations looking for evidence that they are right and that the other person really is 'rude' or 'a nightmare' or 'unhelpful'. Given that we tend to get what we focus on, it's quite likely that the rude, unhelpful, nightmare will make an unwelcome appearance!

Now don't get us wrong. Of course we come across people from time to time who are just downright difficult and nothing we do seems to work. But these people are few and far between.

So the first thing to do is to view any 'challenging' behaviour that you meet as just that ... behaviour. And deal with the behaviour. The key is to be clear what you want to happen and keep heading in that direction.

Let's think then about different types of behaviour and the purpose of that behaviour. If you think about it in broad terms:

- Someone starts to tell you what a rotten day they've had at work. What response are they looking for? (A bit of sympathy)

- Someone shouts at you because you bumped into them. What response are they looking for? (An apology)

- Someone starts complaining about the way the company treats people going on maternity leave. What response are they looking for? (Someone to join in)

- Someone starts to bemoan the state of the nation and how it wasn't like this in their day. What response are they looking for? (Someone to agree with them)

Of course, the exact response will depend on the context, but we hope you get the idea.

The point we want to make here is that, being on the receiving end of this behaviour, **we always have a choice** as to how we respond. We can decide to go along with it providing we're happy with the result it gets us, or we can decide to do something different. Because **'all behaviour has a positive intention'** is as true for us as it is for the people we are communicating with.

So, let's examine two general clusters and the observable behaviours that accompany them, consider what options we have, and work out the best way of dealing with them.

And while we're doing this, just remember that what we've done already, still counts. In other words, keep in mind all the great strategies we've given you already for showing curiosity, listening and building rapport. They're going to be tremendously useful to you when you're dealing with 'challenging' people.

Angry/aggressive

By and large, these behaviours are focused on attracting similar responses. They are looking to 'hook' some kind of compliant response. Clearly they are looking to achieve this in different ways and so their observable behaviour may well be different:

Lots of 'angry' animated movement ⟶ very still

Loud voice, lots or words ⟶ quiet voice, few words

Very expressive, lots of facial expressions ⟶ very few expressions

Very direct eye contact ⟶ looking anywhere but at their 'victim'

These behaviours will vary from person to person but each person will be consistent and predictable. You can probably think of people you know who, when they are getting angry, you can 'spot it coming a mile off'. And once they are angry, they display the same set of behaviours each time.

Critical/patronising/overbearing

We would never want to attribute a particular set of behaviours to any occupation or profession but the fact of the matter is that SOME people in SOME professions resort to SOME of these behaviours and we've all had examples of:

- The Garage Mechanic Syndrome. (Sharp intake of breath followed by pitying look and hollow laugh.)
- The White Coat Approach. (Often accompanied by a stethoscope slung casually around the neck.)
- The 'I've been in this business for 45 years and.....' (It's highly unlikely that anyone alive at this moment in time knows more than I do.)
- The 'The Law just doesn't work that way.' (But only someone with my level of experience and the three degrees I hold would know that.)

- The 'Now then, little lady, this is complicated.....' (This is now implied rather than spoken, because even this person is wary of rabid political incorrectness.)

- The 'We don't give refunds.' (Actually they do because they have to but they reckon you don't know your consumer rights.)

- The 'Leave the Education to the Teachers.' (Having children in no way qualifies you to comment on the way they are taught.)

- This last one, along with 'The Law just doesn't work that way', is a very good example of an over-riding syndrome known as 'The Mystic World Of ... Syndrome'. (Entry to the Mystic World being forbidden except to the chosen and qualified few.)

We're always interested in discovering more, so do let us know if you come across any!

Tears/tantrums/whiners and rebels

Yes, even adults have tantrums. You'll have heard people say, 'Honestly, you'd think they were five years old the way they go on.' And, actually, that's pretty much what they're up to – replicating the behaviour they employed as a child to get the things they wanted. And the interesting thing is that they will continue to display this behaviour as long as it continues to be successful for them.

There can be all sorts of different ways of these manifesting themselves and in spite of some of the terminology we use, these behaviours are equally apparent in men and women, for example:

- the sullen pout
- the flounce
- the 'How dare they treat me like this?'
- the 'Just wait til they ask me for help.'
- the 'No one likes me.'
- the tears on tap.
- the 'I'll get even, don't you worry.'
- the 'They've asked me to work late again. Well, they can whistle.'

This contrasts with:

● The 'They've asked me to work late again. I suppose I'll have to but I don't know what my wife/husband/partner/children will say. It's the fourth time this week and I didn't want to do the other three either.'

You can make up the rest of the cast list yourself.

The question for you is, when faced with these behaviours, what are your options?

A. You can fall into the set of behaviours that will indicate to the other person that they have 'hooked' you.

B. You can respond by displaying similar behaviours yourself.

C. You can decide to display a different set of behaviours that are counter to the other person's expectations.

As you read through the following examples it's useful to think what kind of observable behaviours could accompany them. Behaviour comes in many guises.

Angry/aggressive:

Them: 'I am sick to death of the way you always park your car on my part of the pavement.'

A. **You**: 'I'm really, really sorry, I won't do it again.' (Said in a soft, compliant voice.)

B. **You**: 'It's not YOUR pavement; it belongs to the council.' (Matching the tone and body language of the other person.)

C. **You**: 'It is, though, public land and as such I have a right to park there. I am also concerned about the way you feel about it. Given that, I'd like to resolve it so that we are both happy with the result.' (Using an even tone, few gestures and keeping level eye contact.)

Critical/patronising/overbearing

Them: 'I really think it's best if you leave it ('it' can be anything you like – patient care/child's performance at school/your car problem) to us. We have so much experience in this field.'

A. **You**: 'I know you do. I really wasn't trying to interfere. I was only doing it for the best.' You can probably imagine how the rest of that conversation pans out.

B. **You**: 'Well, that attitude is typical of your profession. I don't know what gives you the right to think you have all the answers.'

C. **You**: 'I recognise that. I also believe that it is my responsibility to keep as closely involved in "it" as I can and I expect you to keep me informed and answer any questions I have.'

Now the language that we use may not suit you, and that's fine. Your job is to work out what does suit you.

So let's think what these different responses entail and what you need to do to be able to give the one that's going to work best for you.

- **Response A** means that you swallow the 'hook' and go along the path laid out by the other person. Now, if that's OK with you, that's fine.

- **Response B** will tend to put you both on a collision course. Some people relish that; the question is whether it gets you where you want to go.

You absolutely **have to remember** in these situations that the key to success is **knowing your outcome**.

- **Response C** clearly comes from another place, another 'state', and is likely to elicit a very different reaction.

We'll christen Response C our **Adult State**. The main thing that distinguishes it from any of the other states – states being identified by the clusters of behaviours that go along with them

– is that it is pretty much an 'emotion-free' state. Whereas, all the other states we've outlined have some kind of emotional power attached to them.

And it is this 'emotion-free' quality that makes the Adult State so powerful. You see, it's very difficult to maintain a high level of emotion if the only response you are getting is 'emotion-free'.

Remember Bill's story that we told you earlier in this chapter? He couldn't keep his emotional out-pouring going. At some point he had to stop.

Even when we come across an apparently less overtly emotional state like 'patronising', the Adult response works really well. Why? Because it doesn't swallow the 'hook'. It has its own innate power, which is best evidenced by the control that goes along with it. By refusing to be overawed or stepping down, the other state has nothing to feed off. You have deprived it of the oxygen it needs to replenish itself. Well done you!

So, in order for you to handle these occasions successfully, we need to give you easy ways to access your Adult State and hold onto it. First off, then, let's look at the characteristics of the Adult State which, in fact, are very similar to those of the state of confidence:

- **posture**: erect, head straight, weight evenly balanced, shoulders relaxed
- **facial expression**: direct eye contact, facial muscles relaxed
- **gestures**: symmetrical, smooth movement, hands relaxed
- **voice**: even tone, middle to lower range of your voice, pausing, measured pace
- **breathing**: regular, deep.

There's a very, very powerful exercise for you on page 157 that will help you to tackle any 'challenging' behaviour.

Handling shy, unforthcoming people

Why would someone decide to be shy? Is it a choice? It certainly is. And behind the choice, as we know by now, lies a positive intention. So, yet again we want to enter any conversation with a shy person by recognising that being shy has some positive consequences for them.

How do you know someone's shy and unforthcoming? You may think, 'It's obvious', and you may well be right. But different people will demonstrate it in different ways and that's the key to having success with them.

Well, we did quite a bit of 'unpacking' of confidence earlier in the book, so let's follow the same route. Shy people are likely to demonstrate at least some of the following characteristics:

- Posture, gesture and eye contact:
    - indirect eye contact
    - less assertive posture
    - head turned away and gaze averted.
- Vocal:
    - quiet voice
    - shallow breathing.
- Verbal:
    - hesitation and pausing
    - lack of questions.

The key to your success with them will be to notice the individual signals and move towards them by matching and pacing. So you may need to:

- give less direct and shorter eye contact
- lower the volume of your voice and speak more slowly
- pause more
- stand at an angle to them rather than face on
- look away more often than you might do normally
- ask questions that demonstrate your interest in them
- ask and talk about other people that you have in common
- acknowledge what they say to you and show interest
- engage in active listening – using 'ah', 'I see', etc., to encourage them to continue

- affirm the fact that you are enjoying being with them
- admit that you feel less than comfortable with new people
- allow time for them to respond to your questions in order to draw them out – avoid filling the silence.

Remember also that this is a very good time to hold on to the beliefs of the great communicators:

- everyone has something unique to offer
- everyone has a story worth telling
- everyone gives me the opportunity to learn something new.

The great thing is that you never know what you're going to find out and it can be very easy to jump to the conclusion that because someone is shy, they have little to offer. It's also worth noting that shyness can sometimes be hidden in different clothes.

Graham's story

A few years ago we worked with a CEO who, in 1:1 meetings and when working with his board of directors, was very personable and charming. His reputation in the business, however, was that he was arrogant and stand-offish.

Finding this very surprising, we asked some of the staff how they knew he was arrogant and they said that when he walked through the offices, he never stopped to talk to anyone and appeared to avoid contact with them.

We talked to Graham about this and he was horrified that the staff thought him arrogant. When we asked him why he walked through the offices without talking to anyone, we hit gold! He was shy.

He didn't know who the people were and in that kind of situation he just clammed up. He was fine 1:1 or with a small group of people that he knew, but outside of that he lost his confidence.

The lesson for us was that you should never assume anything about anyone. And certainly never assume that just because they exhibit one sort of behaviour in one context that it automatically means they will be like that in all contexts.

Standing up for yourself

Standing up for yourself; the phrase says it all. Can you imagine anyone sitting down for themselves?

Control your state with your physiology

Yet again, physiology and state are going to be the keys to us being effective on our own behalf. So let's start by reminding ourselves of the physiology of confidence, which is so closely related to the Adult State. Here's the list we developed earlier:

- Stand up straight.
- Keep your head erect.
- Make good, direct eye contact.
- Adopt and maintain an assertive stance:
  - Stand with your feet hip width apart (this works for both men and women).
  - Keep your weight evenly balanced.
- When walking, walk with purpose.
- Breathe deeply and easily. Breathing deeply from your diaphragm, as opposed to your upper chest, sends a signal to the brain that you are relaxed and confident.
- Use this deep breathing to control your voice.
- Speak slowly, use pauses, enunciate clearly.

It's really important that whatever you do works for you. Often we find with the people we work with that there are one or two behaviours on this list that really make a difference for them.

For example, we worked with one man called Alan for whom simply increasing the volume of his voice – he spoke very softly and quite slowly – had a profound impact on his levels of confidence.

Time then to go 'truffle hunting' on your own behalf. The best way to do this is to try things out. Of course, you can wait til the next time you want to stand up for yourself or start before you need to.

Exercise

Adult State

- Get in front of a mirror; adopt your Adult State physiology
- Notice what a difference changes in posture and stance make to you
- When you see something you like, hold it, associate with it and notice the feelings that go along with it
- Try out different patterns, volumes and rhythms of speech
- Imagine or even practise having a conversation in Adult voice and tone
- Work at it until you're happy with what you see, hear and feel.
- Change physiology and then get back into Adult State again as fast as you can.

You're beginning to get it 'in the muscle'. Do this as many times as you need in order to be confident that you can access it whenever you want. This means that even if you encounter Angry/Aggressive when you are least expecting it, you'll be able to be Adult.

Remember that state drives behaviour and the easiest way to change your state is to change your physiology.

What do all actors do before they go on stage to perform? Rehearse, rehearse, rehearse. And that's exactly what we're encouraging you to do. Rehearse success.

And for anyone who feels there is something false about this, who thinks, 'But I'm not an actor', please consider this. Ever since you were a baby you have been learning from others in order to become the person you are today. When you were tiny you modelled your behaviour from the people around you; your parents, your family, people you looked up to.

All we're asking you to do now is to continue your learning and to model the behaviours of those people who are really successful and effective communicators. And even if you don't feel completely confident, act 'as if' you are confident. It works. How? Well, here's the thing. Act 'as if' often enough, and before you know what's happened you've learnt a new set of behaviours that will stay with you for life.

Be assertive – Adult rules, OK?

When you stand up for yourself, stand up as an adult and in your Adult State. Remember what we talked about when we were discussing handling angry/aggressive behaviour. The best possible state to be in when standing up for yourself is the Adult State. In this state you take the emotion out of the situation and respond to whatever stimulus is provided by remaining logical, factual and direct. This is the key difference between being assertive and aggressive. Aggression contains emotion and emotion has no part to play in an assertive conversation.

Of course, you may be feeling emotional about the issue but you do not reflect this in your behaviour. And that means you may need to prepare yourself. In fact, unless the situation hits you without warning, then you must make every effort to prepare yourself.

Be assertive – prepare the ground

Let's assume you have a conversation coming up where you need to stand up for yourself and you want to be well prepared for it. There is a native American saying, 'Never judge a man until you have walked a mile in his moccasins'. When we have to stand up for ourselves, when we come under attack, or when we have to defend our corner, we can be drawn into seeing things only from our own perspective. How often have you heard people say things like:

'I'm going to put them right.'

'It's all their fault.'

'They never see it my way.'

'I'll show them what's what.'

'They just don't get it, they never do.'

Of course it's important for us to get our point across, but the most productive conversations are those that happen when there is some sense of balance to them. The people quoted above have all their thinking on one side of the argument. In other words, it's unbalanced.

Sometimes it's very difficult to see the other person's perspective; sometimes, if we're honest with ourselves, we just don't want to. We find ourselves thinking, 'Why on earth should I think about it from their angle; they would never do that for me.'

If this ever happens to you, just remember:

"The person with the most flexibility in any relationship will be the catalyst for change."

Here's the first terrific strategy for preparing for your conversation.

The three positions

Think, if you can, about a conversation that you have coming up where you are going to have to stand up for yourself. If you haven't got one, then think of one that you had in the past.

You're going to experience this situation from three different positions. Before you apply these to the conversation, we'll explain the three positions:

First position

From this position you see, hear and feel the situation from your own perspective. You think about what you want, what your outcomes are, what is important to you. If you were to describe the situation, you would use 'I', demonstrating that you are seeing everything from your own point of view:

'I want ...'

'I feel ...'

'I think ...'

'I see ...'

'As far as I am concerned ...'

This position is really useful when you want to stand up for yourself. You can adopt this position to help you to decide what it is you really want and to rehearse yourself getting it. It is a great position from which to develop assertive behaviour.

On the other hand, over-emphasis on first-position thinking can lead to a disregard for others. You may have met people who see things only from their own point of view and find it difficult, if not impossible, to appreciate anyone else's. They can be entirely dismissive of other people's suggestions and pay little regard to other people's feelings.

Second position

From this position you see, hear and feel the situation from the other person's perspective. Your aim is to experience the situation as if you were them. When you describe the situation in second position, keep using 'I' since you are, for the time being, the other person.

Remember that **'all behaviour has a positive intention'**. Taking up this position and really associating with it can help you to see the other person's point of view and can lead to a real understanding of the positive intentions that may be driving their behaviour. This position will also help you to develop different ways of approaching the other person based on your increased understanding of their experience of the situation.

Is there a downside? The downside lies in over-identification with another. You may well have met people who always put other people's needs and wants first at the expense of their own. They continually back down in the face of opposition to their views and never assert themselves.

The worst case scenario is that they take on other people's feelings to the extent that they completely dominate their lives. In fact they have no 'life of their own'.

Third position

From this position you look at the situation as if you were an impartial observer. You see and hear both parties as if you were a third person. Since you are separating yourself from the situation, you will have access to your Adult State and you will find that you experience much less, if any, emotional content. This means that you will be able to consider courses of action more effectively and easily.

The downside of over-use of third position is a lack of emotional attachment. People who spend the majority of their time in third position can give the impression of not being interested or engaged. They can appear impervious to other people's emotional reactions and can come across as uncaring.

Tip: When you do the exercise, find three different physical spaces for the different positions. So, if you want to do the exercise sitting down, have three different chairs for first, second and third positions. Sit in each of them so that you experience the situation differently physiologically.

If you want to do the exercise standing up, then simply create three different positions in the room.

Exercise

The Three Chairs – applying the three positions

In order to get the best out of this exercise, make sure that you put aside some time when you will be free from interruptions.

Think of the conversation that you are anticipating having.

First position

Firstly, think through what you want from the conversation. Set yourself a positive outcome and consider the positive consequences of getting it. (Revisit Chapter 1 if you need to.)

Next take yourself to the time of the conversation so that you are there and experience how you feel. Hold your outcome in your mind all the time.

Now start to make any alterations you may need to make to ensure that you have a balanced and positive internal representation of the event. Create a picture that has the characteristics that trigger a positive state in you:

- put yourself on the same level as the other person – if you imagine the other person as being larger than you, speaking with a louder voice than you, it is more of a challenge to behave assertively

- have level, direct, eye contact

- speak at the same volume

- create your own, calm, positive feelings.

Conduct the conversation in the way that you want it to unfold. Imagine it reaching the conclusion that you want.

Second position

Change positions as we have suggested above. Fully associate with the other person in order to see the situation from their point of view.

Think how they behave; consider their posture; think how they speak and what they say. Match their behaviour, their posture.

What did you notice in this position? What insights do you gain? What feelings do you experience?

Then go through the same process as you have in first position so that you create a balanced and positive internal representation of the event.

Third position

Now stand back and view the situation from third position. Notice what happens and where you see any imbalance in the picture adjust it so that you achieve equality:

- Are the two people ('you' and the other person) physically balanced – on the same level, matching posture?
- Is the sound – volume, tonality – balanced?

Also notice what feelings you have, if any, in this position. If you do, then identify to whom those feelings belong, and give them back to the appropriate person. Remove yourself from the emotion.

Final step

Move back into first position and notice now how you experience the situation now:

- you will notice that you have discovered new information
- You will have a greater level of understanding of the other person's perspective
- You will have clarity about what you want to achieve
- You will have more choices available to you in the way in which you approach the situation.

If you feel the need to make any more adjustments, then simply repeat the process. As with any new skill, the more often you practise it, the easier it will become.

How to put your case

We've already made the point that preparation is the key to success and this next strategy is a very simple and powerful four-point framework for assertive conversations. It is the **DESC Framework.** We'll explain each part of the framework and then give you a couple of examples of **DESC** in action.

Describe: you describe the issue or situation that is causing you concern.

Explain: you explain the impact that the issue is having on you.

Specify: you specify what you want or what you want to be different.

Consequences: you outline the positive consequences of you achieving your outcome and, if appropriate, the negative consequences of you not achieving it.

Example 1: Social

D: 'You told me that we would work together on the arrangements for John's birthday party but you have gone ahead and done it yourself without consulting me.'

E: 'I want you to know that this has made me feel angry and ignored.'

S: 'I realise it is too late to change anything this time but next year I expect you to include me in all the planning from the word "Go".'

C: 'If you do, then I will happily take on the lion's share of the catering myself. If you don't then I will assume you are happy to bear all the costs yourself in future.'

Example 2: Work

D: 'You've asked me to work late on six occasions in the last two weeks.'

E: 'Whilst I'm happy to put in extra time every so often, this has become so regular that it is having a real impact on my home life and my children.'

S: 'I will still continue to work late, but I want to limit it to no more than one day a week.'

C: 'If you want time over and above that then you will have to find someone else, whose family is less dependent on them, to do it.'

Example 3: Making a complaint

D: 'I brought my car in to have the steering fixed two weeks ago for the third time and it is quite clear from the way that it's handling that you still have not sorted out the problem.'

E: 'I am very concerned that it is endangering myself and my family. As a result I cannot use it with them and that means that I am having real problems getting them around.'

S: 'I want you to take it back now, resolve the issue and in the meantime, because I will be without transport, I will expect you to provide me with a courtesy car. I will not expect you to charge me again for the work you do.'

C: 'On the basis that you do all this, I will be happy to continue to use you. If you are not able to accommodate me then I will appeal directly to the manufacturer, citing the poor service you have given me.'

Again, we appreciate that the language in these examples may not match the way in which you might phrase your requests and that's fine. Just adapt it to your style while you hang on to the framework.

What this will help you to do is take the emotion out of the conversation and keep you in your Adult State.

Tip: Give yourself time to script your response and to practise it.

Chapter

7

When to shut up!

So far we've given you a whole range of great strategies to introduce you into conversations; to keep you talking; to make you the centre of attention; to enable you to build great relationships; to help you deal effectively with difficult situations and to ensure that you shine when you want to.

So it may seem a bit odd to introduce a chapter that teaches you how and when to shut up! But, believe us, shutting up at the right time is as important a skill as any other.

- Have you ever been talking to someone and wished they would stop?
- Have you ever cringed when someone has gone just that bit (or maybe even way) too far?
- Have you ever wished the ground would swallow you up when you realised that you had done the same thing?

Well, if you have ever had any of those experiences and you don't want to have them again, you've come to the right place.

Why do it?

Why exactly do people keep on talking when they should shut up? There are a number of reasons:

- they are impervious to the effect they're having on other people
- they are nervous and can't stop babbling on
- they keep repeating themselves
- they can't stand silence and feel a need to fill it
- they want to help when the best way of helping would be silence.

We're going to tackle these one by one.

They are impervious to the effect they're having on other people

This is a tough one since it raises the question as to how, if you are impervious to the effect you're having, you would notice! So if you are one of these people, you probably don't even know that you are.

Assuming then that you don't know but just in case you might on occasion be one, here are some techniques to help you become aware.

Most people who just go on and on in this way will tend to be occupying first position – you can refer back to Chapter 6 to remind yourself – and will be so focused on their own experience as to be oblivious to others.

The first thing to do, and something to practise regularly, is to start to notice what reactions you are getting from those around you. Think for a moment:

● How do you know that people are listening to you?
● What do people look like when they are engaged in what another person is saying?
● What kind of reactions do you expect from people who are interested in you?
● What do you do yourself to express interest in someone else?

The clues for you will be in the verbal, vocal and non-verbal reactions that you are getting. So, as you talk, start to notice what is happening in front of you:

● Are people maintaining eye contact with you?
● Are they looking at you as they react to you or are they looking away?
● Are they asking you questions that demonstrate that they have listened to you?
● Take a pause and notice what happens. Does someone change the subject or do they pursue the topic of your conversation?
● When you pause do they make to move away or do they keep comfortably in contact with you?

Besides anything else this is great practice for becoming more self-aware. It also helps you to make the transition from over-emphasis on first position to a more balanced view of the world and an appreciation of other people's point of view.

They are nervous and can't stop babbling on

We've already spent some time on getting rid of anxiety before attending a social event, but sometimes nerves creep up on us and catch us unawares. What to do then?

The secret lies in your breathing. Since one of the first symptoms of nerves is the shift of breathing to the upper chest which results in shortness of breath and the consequent effect on our speech, that should become the focus of our attention.

Slow your breathing down and concentrate on moving it to the lower part of your tummy. As you do this you will automatically slow your rate of speech. You can then turn your attention to the people around you and engage fully with them. This has the effect of shifting your focus of attention from inside to outside. Once you have achieved this, you will notice all signs of nerves have gone.

Remember that if you are fully concentrating – listening with ears, eyes and heart – on other people, it is impossible to be focused on yourself. And it is the focus on self that creates the state of nervousness.

They keep repeating themselves

Repetition is another symptom of nervousness and so the same techniques we discussed above will work equally well. Since most of us who tend to repeat ourselves are conscious of what we're doing, there are two other strategies we can employ:

1. Stop yourself. If you notice that you are repeating yourself just say 'Stop' to yourself and stop!
2. Get others to stop you. Ask friends and acquaintances to step in if you start to repeat yourself or every so often throw in the request/question, 'Please stop me if I've told you this already' or 'Have I already told you this?'

They can't stand silence and feel a need to fill it

The 'silence fillers' amongst us are very definitely adept at second position. More often than not their desire to fill the silence is based, not only on their own awkwardness but also on their perception (sometimes accurate, sometimes not – commonly known as mind reading) of the awkwardness of others.

The key here is to become comfortable with silence. That doesn't mean you need to stand there for half an hour with no one speaking; it just means that a few moments' silence in a conversation is natural, as natural as breathing.

You'll no doubt be able to recall many instances of 'comfortable silences' with friends. So when a silence occurs:

- remember it isn't your job to break it; other people are involved
- it may just be that the conversation has reached its natural conclusion; it's time to move on
- take the time to re-run the conversation to date – this may give you an ideal starting point for a new conversation
- think about who you're with and pick up on a subject that you have in common for re-starting the conversation
- if you're with people or a person you don't know that well you can always use the silence as an opportunity to move to another group/person saying something like:

'I've really enjoyed talking with you. There is someone else I want to meet, so if you'll forgive me I'll see if I can find them.'

'I've really enjoyed our chat. Time for me to find another drink. Can I get you one?'

They want to help when the best way of helping would be silence

This is another very good example of 'all behaviour has a positive intention'.

But have you ever had the experience of wanting to talk, maybe to unburden yourself and the person you're with, probably a friend, has butted in as they try to help you?

We are, by and large, 'solution seeking missiles'. (We don't want to appear sexist at this juncture, but this does apply more to men than to women!) We tend to find it quite a challenge to not offer help and what we see as potential solutions to a problem, especially if we think it will be helpful to someone we care about.

If you realise you are prone to this, then the solution is really very simple. Ask what would be the best thing you could do to help. This at least gives the other person the chance to say, 'Just listen.'

Many of us have learned the hard way that advice is not always wanted and that our ears, eyes and heart will do nicely, thank you.

Chapter

8

How to talk when you want to shine

There are probably going to be certain occasions when you really want to shine. That's not to say that you don't want to be able to talk with confidence all the time; it's just that there are some occasions when you want to be able to be even more confident and come across in a way that really marks you out.

These occasions can sometimes turn out to be life-changing events, such as:

- job interviews
- going out on a date
- meeting with an extremely important client
- pitching for a vital piece of business
- meeting your future in-laws for the first time!

In this chapter we're going to look at some of the strategies you can employ at times like these.

We've already covered some of these strategies separately in previous chapters and now is the time to bring everything together to really turbo-charge your confidence.

Whilst all the events we've listed above are different in terms of their context, we're going to give you the strategies here that will work for any of those events. So all you need to do is to adapt them to the particular situation you are going to find yourself in.

Shine secret 1: the power of you

In Chapter 2 we showed you how to build up a really confident state by creating the 'future you'. Whenever you have an event coming up when you really want to shine these exercises should be part of your preparation.

Whether you're going out on a date, to a client's offices, or to your prospective in-laws doesn't matter. Here's your blueprint for successful preparation:

- Find out whatever you can about the place you're going to so that you can do your mental rehearsal in some detail.

- Decide how you want to come across, what impression you want to make.

- Find out whatever you can about what's important to the person or people you're meeting.

- If you're going on a blind date and you discover your date is interested in mountain biking, do your research and find out something about it. This means that you will be able to build very quick rapport by using the right language and terminology. (If you hate physical activity you might decide to call it off!)

- Decide what's important to you about this meeting and what you want to get from it.

- It may seem like a blinding glimpse of the obvious but if you're going for an interview or to pitch for business, make sure you've done your research on the company concerned and the people you're going to meet.

Tim remembers going for an interview some years ago and completely blowing his interviewer away when he slipped into the conversation two or three facts about him that he had discovered during his research. He got the job.

- If you are going for an interview, make sure that you prepare some really great open questions to ask.

Once you've done all this you're ready to do the 'future you' exercise on page 26 adapted to the particular situation. Give yourself enough time, make sure you're not going to be disturbed and rehearse it til you're happy that you can run it through in a moment whenever you want to.

Shine secret 2: the power of your body

Remember how powerful you are and how quickly people leap to judgement. This checklist will serve you well:

- be dressed appropriately for the occasion
- make sure you are well groomed
- make sure you are clean
- walk with purpose
- greet people with a smile
- have a firm handshake
- speak audibly and clearly
- look people in the eye
- stand still when others are speaking
- don't fidget
- listen intently to what people are saying.

Some things to emphasise when you want to shine are the following:

- **Eye contact:** Remember that of all the non verbal signals we use, eye contact is the one that people pay most attention to when making their unconscious decisions about how confident we are. This is true on a 1:1 or 1:group basis. There is no surer way of winning someone over than with great eye contact. More than demonstrating confidence it shows interest and is one of the main proofs of our listening. If you want to make a great impression on your date, use dynamic eye contact. Make them the sole focus of your attention.

- **Smile:** Smiles open doors. Doors into conversations and doors into hearts. Never underestimate the power of a genuine smile. Whenever you want to connect with someone on first meeting, shake hands firmly and as you look at them allow your smile to arrive.

- **Posture:** Keep your posture 'open'. By that we mean adopt a posture that is welcoming to others. Stand with your legs apart and your feet turned slightly outwards. Keep your hands relaxed and avoid crossing your arms. Whilst it may be comfortable for you, it can give the impression of you being 'closed off'.

Shine secret 3: the power of pacing

We want to reinforce here the power of matching and pacing. We spent a good deal of time looking at this together in Chapter 4.

Always remember that 'people like people like them'. The closer you can get into their world, the more people will be drawn to you. And most of this will happen at an unconscious level.

Let us give you a personal example:

Emma and Tim's story

When we met some fourteen years ago, both of us were already in relationships, so our decision to get together created some havoc. The fact that Tim had already been married twice and had four children didn't really help Emma's parents to see our relationship in a particularly positive light!

One day, fairly early on, Emma was talking to her father, Michael, about things. She was hoping to convince him that we had both found the person we had been looking for and that everything was going to be OK. He was, of course, very concerned for her.

Michael used to race saloon cars. He retains his love of the sport. At one particular moment he turned to Emma and said:

'Look, if you were offered a racing car that you knew kept coming off the track at a particular point on the circuit and crashing, how likely is it that you would decide it was a good buy?'

Emma's response is worthy of an entry in the annals of pacing.

'Yes, I can see that. But what if a very, very skilled mechanic got hold of it and fixed the fault so that it never crashed again. How would that be?'

'Ah well, that would be all right', said Michael. And that was the last time he ever exhibited any concern about our relationship.

"Never underestimate the power of pacing."

Shine secret 4: the power of your language

Confident people use confident language. And that means positive language.

It's a good exercise to listen to your language for a while and find out what kind of language you are using unconsciously. Listen to others around you and get used to hearing how they express their internal levels of confidence in the language they use.

Examples of positive language:

'We can do this.' vs 'We might be able to get it done.'

'I'm certain I'll enjoy the party.' vs 'I hope it's going to be OK.'

'You look great tonight.' vs 'I quite like that dress.' (Beware flying footwear!)

'I know we can deliver the solution you need.' vs 'Hopefully we'll be able to do that for you.'

'I'm a very reliable person.' vs 'I always try to get in on time.'

Words to avoid:

'Try' – implies the possibility of failure.

'But' – they used to have a saying in one company we worked for that, 'Everything before the "but" is b******t'. A great strategy here is to turn every 'but' into 'and'. Give it a go and see what happens. For example, look at the difference between these two statements:

'I hear what you say but I think we ought to look at it again.'

'I hear what you say and I think looking at it again would give us even more options.'

Shine secret 5: the power of 'we'

If you want to build a relationship quickly then one of the most powerful words to use is 'We'.

You'll remember that in Chapter 3 we worked together using the iceberg as a metaphor for getting below the surface. Above the surface is what YOU know about THEM. When you get below the surface you move to a different level of relationship, a level of understanding. And people who understand each other start to talk about 'we' because 'we' understand each other, don't 'we'?

So if you want to take a short cut you can go straight to 'We' which assumes that you already have a level of understanding and relationship, even though you may only just have met.

The other words that you can then use naturally are 'us', 'our', 'ours'.

Shine secret 6: the power of listening and questioning

From the work we did in Chapter 3 you know already that questioning, if done well, is one of the great ways of becoming interesting:

"Being interested makes you interesting!"

Open and closed questions are second nature to you now so it's time to develop your skills even further so that you can talk to everyone in complete confidence. You'll always know what question to ask next and that will make you shine.

We just need to emphasise here that in order to ask brilliant questions, you do have to listen brilliantly as well.

A quick piece of revision

In Chapter 3 we introduced you to the Process of Communication. We showed you how we use the processes of Deletion, Distortion and Generalisation and that one of the filters that we all use is language. The result of all of this is that when we recount our experiences of an event we apply these processes and filters to that description. Hence the reason that you can attend the same event as someone else and when they describe it, wonder whether you were both in the same place at the same time!

Well of course you were at the same event; it's just that you were seeing it from very different perspectives.

We don't describe the event completely. We select unconsciously the pieces to remember and then choose the language we want to describe it. And now we're back to the iceberg. You can imagine that the language we use is the bit 'above the waterline'. To find out more we need to go 'below the waterline' just as we did in Chapter 3, only now we're going to concentrate on the language the other person is using to guide us. And in order to do this we need to listen really well.

What are we listening for? Well, we're listening for the Deletions, Distortions and Generalisations so that we can use these as springboards for our questions.

Let's look at an example:

John's story

John, a financial adviser, met a new client for a meeting and from the word go could feel there was some kind of tension in the air. John asked the client if anything was wrong and he said, 'I'm afraid I'm not going to be your easiest client. You see, I think deep down that all financial advisers are out to rip me off.'

John decided to go 'truffle hunting' and discovered that on **one** occasion, a few years previously, **one** financial adviser had given his client a piece of bad advice which had cost him a lot of money.

What had the client done? He had **generalised** that experience to cover **all** financial advisers.

What John had done was to spot the generalisation and instead of jumping to the defence of financial advisers, questioned the generalisation to discover what lay 'under the waterline'.

Now, knowing how his client felt and also knowing that his negative view stemmed from one instance, John was able to handle the issue by following a very simple, powerful structure:

- listen – remember; ears, eyes and heart
- empathise – explain that you understand how the person must feel/have felt
- question – make sure you have **all** the information relating to the issue and an understanding of what the other person needs and wants
- solution – propose what you intend to do that meets the other person's needs
- agree – how things are going to work from now on.

If there's one thing that is absolutely vital to hang on to in this structure, it's the bit about finding out what the other person needs and wants to happen, and here's why!

Have you ever been in the situation with someone where you've been trying to be really helpful and you've found yourself offering them what you think is a great solution, only for them to turn round and say, 'No, that won't work' or 'I've tried that already'?

You may even have been in the position where someone you've been sharing a problem with started firing possible solutions at you and you found yourself thinking, 'If only they'd let me finish' or 'I don't want their solutions, I just want to talk about it.'

If you've ever experienced anything like this, you've either been in the presence of, or become yourself, a **Solution Seeking Missile!** And it's all done with a really positive intention. We like helping people. We like to think that where they can't see the wood for the trees, our laser-like intelligence has quickly identified the best course of action.

Please pause and wait until you know what the other person wants. Do this and then provide a solution that fits the bill and you will be the most popular person around.

And if you are reading this and have any kind of sales background, you will know that this is, bar none, the most effective approach to selling. It's an interesting fact, though, that very few sales people do this!

Now, we weren't at the meeting with John and his client but he might, using the structure we've given you, have said something like this:

John's story – continued

'I think I know how you must have felt. [**Empathy**] I know people/ have clients who have had similar experiences [as long as he has]. What I want to do is find out [questions coming] exactly what I need to do to ensure that you have the confidence to work with me and to alleviate any concerns you have about that.'
[**Understanding Needs and Wants**]

▶

'Once I know that, then I can put everything in place [**Solution**] that will give you the confidence to proceed. How does that sound to you?'[**Looking for Agreement**]

Now, on the way to this you need to be paying really good attention to what the other person is saying and here are some very specific examples in the following table that will help you to identify the kind of words and phrases to listen out for that will give you the chance to become really interested and to shine.

	When you hear ...	Ask ...
1	Most/Too Better/Best Worse/Worst Hard/Easy Good/Bad	*According to whom?* *By what criteria?* *What evidence do you have?* *Compared to what?*
2	Unspecified *Noun*	*What **Noun**, specifically?*
3	Them/They We/Us/Our	*Who are them/they/we/us.* *Specifically?*
4	Unspecified *Verb*	*How **Verb**, specifically?*
5	Should Must Have to Ought to	*What would happen if you didn't?* *or* *According to whom?*
6	Shouldn't Mustn't Can't Impossible	*What would happen if you did?* *OR* *What stops you?*
7	Always/Never All/Every No-one	*Always? (exaggerate)* *OR* *Has there ever been a time when..?*

Here are examples of each of the seven classes set out in the above table:

1. 'That Italian restaurant is the best around.'
   'In what way best?' or 'Compared with what?'

2. 'The service in that shop is the pits.'
   'What kind of service are you talking about?'

3. 'They do nothing to help.'
   'Who does nothing?' or 'Who do you mean?'

4. 'She completely ignored me.'
   'How exactly did she ignore you?'

5. 'It's no good. I've got to stay late again tomorrow.'
   'What would happen if you didn't?'

   Or

   'I really ought to go to the party, I suppose.'

   'What would happen if you didn't?'

6. 'I just can't seem to get the kind of job I want.'
   'What stops you?'

   Or

   'I can't ask her out.'

   'What would happen if you did?'

7. 'No one ever says thanks me around here.'
   'No one?' or 'Has anyone ever said thanks?'

   Or

   'We always end up doing all the cooking.'
   'Always?'

Tip: As with everything we've said so far, take it easy and start to listen closely to what people say. You'll be amazed at the amount of information you can gain and the things you can find out about people just by giving them your undivided attention.

Shine strategy 7: the power of confidence

You know something? You have enough great strategies now to talk to everyone with confidence. You have all you need to shine. The only extra ingredient is simply having the confidence to put it all into action. And here's the great thing about all this:

"Putting it into action will give you the confidence you need."

You have our full permission to approach any stranger, go out on any date, walk into any interview, face any difficult situation and be extraordinarily successful!

Let these words from **Nelson Mandela** spur you on:

Our deepest fear is not that we are inadequate.
Our deepest fear is that we are powerful beyond measure.
It is our light, not our darkness, that most frightens us.
We ask ourselves:
Who am I to be brilliant, gorgeous, talented and fabulous?
Actually, who are you not to be?
You are a child of the universe.
Your playing small doesn't serve the world.
There is nothing enlightening about shrinking so that
other people won't feel insecure around you.
We are born to manifest the glory of the universe that is within us.
It is not just in some of us: it is in everyone.
And as we let our light shine,
We unconsciously give other people permission to do the same.
And as we are liberated from our own fear,
Our presence automatically liberates others.

Nelson Mandela – 1994 Inaugural Speech

ARGUING WELL IS AN ART – DISCOVER HOW YOU CAN DO IT BETTER

The ability to persuade, influence and convince is a vital skill for success in work and life. However, most of us have little idea how to argue well. Indeed, arguing is still seen by many as something to be avoided at all costs, and mostly it's done really badly – or not at all. Yet it's possibly the most powerful and yet most neglected asset you could have.

Take control and lead the life you want to live.

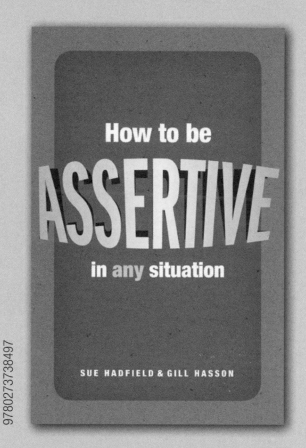

Discover life-changing techniques to help challenge your fears, grow self-confidence and steer your life in the direction you want to go. Whether you are stuck in a rut, looking to make a big change or you want to put more of you into what you do, this book will give you the tools to build a happy and fulfilling life.